DATE DUE

BETTER THAN LIFE

BETTER THAN LIFE

TODAY'S STORIES OF FAITH AT ANY COST

Discovery House Publishers

Books, music, and videos that feed the soul with the Word of God

Box 3566 Grand Rapids, MI 49501

Discovery House Publishers is affiliated with RBC Ministries, Grand Rapids, Michigan.

Discovery House Books are distributed to the trade exclusively by Barbour Publishing, Inc., Uhrichsville, Ohio.

Requests for permission to quote from this book should be directed to: Permissions Department, Discovery House Publishers, P.O. Box 3566, Grand Rapids, MI 49501.

Lyrics for "Better Than Life," "These Scars," "My Heart Will Sing," and "The Pleasure of My King" by Shannon Wexelberg, © 2007 Shanny Banny Music/BMI, are used by permission of Discovery House Music. Lyrics for "Pray" by Scott Krippayne, © 2007 by Purple Honda Music/ASCAP, are used by permission of Discovery House Music.

Unless otherwise indicated, Scripture quotations are from the *Holy Bible, New International Version®. NIV®.* Copyright ©1973, 1978, 1984 by International Bible Society. Used by permission of Zondervan. All rights reserved.

Interior design by Nicholas Richardson

Printed in the United States of America
07 08 09 10 11/ CHG /10 9 8 7 6 5 4 3 2 1

Foreword

Suffering incredibly, the old Christian patriarch finally gave in to the evil tortures of his tormenters. A teenage girl, part of the congregation being forced to watch, jumped to her feet and cried out, "No, no—do not deny now what you have so faithfully proved to believe. These tortures will soon be over. Better to die than deny our Lord whom you have so faithfully served!"

The young woman's pleas brought the old saint back to his senses. He begged forgiveness for his weakness and then beseeched his tormenters to finish their terrible tortures. They did. The teenager was then stripped, raped, and killed for her courageous stand.

I remember this story from my first reading of *Fox's Book of Martyrs* because it made a powerful impression on me. The testimonies of others who have been persecuted and martyred have also marked me: medical missionary Dr.

Carlson, killed in the Congo in 1965; my Waodani Indian friend from Ecuador, Tonae, a Waengongi Ponenani ("God follower") who was speared by his own relatives when he refused to help them in a revenge killing raid against another Waodani clan; Gracia Burnham, a New Tribes missionary serving in the Philippines, who, with her husband Martin, was held hostage by guerrillas for a year before she was injured and Martin was killed in a gun battle in 2002; missionary Jim Bowers, whose wife Ronnie and baby daughter Charity were killed when their plane was shot down by our own CIA and the Peruvian Air Force in 2001. These God-followers' pain and heroic faith have anchored my own resolve to persevere.

One story of martyrdom that has affected me even more than these is an incident involving a group of five young missionaries who were killed in 1956 in Ecuador. A group of Waodoni Indians brutally attacked the men as they attempted to share the gospel with them. One of those young men was my father, Nate Saint. But God used these five "seeds" to fill the rosters of mission agencies with candidates who wanted to be just like my dad and the others who died with him: Jim Elliot, Ed McCully, Pete Fleming, and Roger Youderian. You see, God does work in mysterious ways.

So what do we do about persecution? I suggest that we don't need to look for it. It will find us if we truly pattern our lives after Christ. No, we don't yearn for it, but neither should we despair over it. Jesus told us, "You are blessed when you are reviled and persecuted . . . for God's sake. Celebrate and be glad because your reward in heaven is so worth the pain (Matthew 5:11–12, own paraphrase).

Enduring pain for God's sake is a wonderful agony, a unique opportunity to be used by God. It is part of God's plan to turn what man means for evil into an irresistible force for good. That is why Paul said, "We are afflicted in every way, but not crushed; perplexed, but not despairing; persecuted, but not forsaken; struck down, but not destroyed" (2 Corinthians 4:8–9 NASB).

There are really two questions we need to ask ourselves. First, what do we do if and when we face persecution? To that I say with confidence, get ready to see God manifest Himself in ways you have not experienced before. We know that God is able to miraculously deliver us as Shadrach, Meshach, and Abednego testified. But if He should choose not to, then He will give us the courage, like He did those three brave men, to declare, "But even if He doesn't, we still won't serve your gods." Why? Because they trusted their

God (Daniel 3:17, own paraphrase). Job said it best: "Shall we accept only good things from the hand of God and never anything bad?" (2:10 NLT).

The second and more pertinent question we should ask ourselves with extreme care is what do we do about the suffering of our persecuted brothers and sisters? We must stand with them. We certainly have to pray for them. Like the young teenage girl, we should join with them in their suffering at times. We need to prepare ourselves with faith, should that be the answer. And there are times when our outrage might deliver them from their suffering. But, above all else, we must understand that God does work in mysterious ways. We must not stand in the way of His redeeming acts, even when it brings suffering to ourselves and those we love.

We are His servants, not He ours. So take courage, brothers and sisters. "Be steadfast, immovable, always abounding in the work of the Lord, knowing that your toil is not in vain in the Lord" (1 Corinthians 15:58 NASB).

STEVE SAINT

August 2007

Introduction

Christians in countries like North Korea, Eritrea, Saudi Arabia, China, Pakistan, and Turkey understand the reality of what the apostle Paul was talking about in Philippians 3:10. These nations are among the worst persecutors of Christians, and believers living in them are all too frequently called to "know Christ . . . and the fellowship of sharing in his sufferings."

Believers in countries that celebrate religious freedom get up in the morning, say goodbye to their families, go off to work, and perhaps attend a Bible study in the evening with the reasonable expectation that they will experience the same routine tomorrow. But believers living in countries and among cultures that are hostile to the gospel get up in the morning, say goodbye to their families, go off to work, and perhaps attend a Bible study with the reasonable expectation that they may be arrested before noon. By the end of the day, they may have been beaten for sharing their faith with a neighbor. An extremist who hates them for being a Christian may execute them while they wait for public transportation or attend a meeting with fellow workers. Perhaps these sound like exaggerated situations that could never occur in real life—but they have.

We shouldn't be surprised that Christians suffer for their faith in the twenty-first century. Jesus told His disciples, "If the world hates you, keep in mind that it hated me first . . . You do not belong to the world, but I have chosen you out of the world. That is why the world hates you" (John 15:18–19). Jesus goes on to say that His servants shouldn't expect to be treated any better than He was treated. He was persecuted, and if we obey His teachings, we will be as well.

It is difficult for us to imagine how there can be anything good about persecution. Yet Scripture and the testimony of those who have shared in Christ's sufferings reveal that the persecution of God's people can serve His purposes. Following the death of Stephen, the first New Testament martyr, "a great persecution broke out against the church at Jerusalem," and Christians, carrying the gospel message with them, "scattered throughout Judea and Samaria" (Acts 8:1). One eyewitness of this execution—a young man named

Saul—heard Stephen's prayer of forgiveness as he died. This eyewitness came to be known as the apostle Paul, a powerful proponent of the gospel and eventual martyr himself. Like Stephen, Susanne Geske, wife of martyr Tilmann Geske, expressed her forgiveness to her husband's killers in a television interview in April 2007. Living in Turkey among people who perceive revenge as acceptable and expected, Susanne has changed lives with her words. One columnist wrote, "She said in one sentence what a thousand missionaries in a thousand years could never do."

Another interesting thing that Jesus teaches us about persecution is that those who experience it are blessed: "Blessed are those who are persecuted because of righteousness, for theirs is the kingdom of heaven" (Matthew 5:10). In testimony after testimony, persecuted Christians speak of the joy and peace they experience as they suffer for Christ's sake. The apostle Peter explains the reason for this joy: "Rejoice that you participate in the sufferings of Christ, so that you may be overjoyed when his glory is revealed" (1 Peter 4:13). An imprisoned Christian shares the gospel with his or her cellmates, leading some to Christ; a martyr's family members extend forgiveness to those who have murdered their loved one; Christians who hear of the suffering of others commit their own lives to being enthusiastic bearers of the gospel message—in all of these ways Christ's glory is revealed, and His people rejoice.

How do we who experience religious freedom respond to the plight of our brothers and sisters who experience daily oppression for their faith? We must pray—for strength and courage for those who are suffering, for protection for those in oppressive countries so that they can continue to share the gospel, and for opportunities for those who have been persecuted to share their faith. Perhaps most difficult of all, we must pray "for those who persecute" (Matthew 5:44), that they may come to know the gospel of peace as well. There are other ways that you can help persecuted believers, and you can find out how to offer support by contacting the organizations listed at the back of the book.

It is our hope at Discovery House Publishers that Christ's glory will be revealed as we share these stories of faith at any cost and that you will be blessed and encouraged to "consider it pure joy whenever you face trials" (James 1:2).

BETTER THAN LIFE

This world has left me here with nothing
Took my silver and my gold
But there's one thing they can't take from me
This treasure that I hold

You've made me rich in grace and mercy
Now my heart is satisfied
So let them take my whole life from me
It is worth the price

Your love is better than life
Better than life
Oh, Lord
So much better than life

Tell me, what can this world offer
That can make the broken whole
For there is just one living water
That fills the empty soul

So I declare to earth and heaven
That I have chosen to believe
And oh, the riches I've been given
They overflow to me

My lips will praise You
My soul will bless Your name
My heart will trust in You, my Lord
Your cross before me
Your word alive within me
I will boast in You alone

SHANNON J. WEXELBERG,
FROM THE CD *BETTER THAN LIFE*

Better Than Life

Because your love is better than life, my lips will glorify you.

PSALM 63:3

Santosh grew up in India, the oldest of nine children in a poor Dalit family. Often called Untouchables, the Dalits fall below the bottom rung of the infamous Indian caste structure and are considered less than human. Dalits do not have adequate access to food, housing, clothing, education, or health care. Suffering, discrimination, oppression—these mark the life of a Dalit.

As one of these "broken" people, Santosh knew only of his own village traditions and mindset. He had little education, and his parents married him off at a young age, a common tribal custom. He became a blacksmith, crafting iron tools used in homes and on farms. Like most people in his village, Santosh worshiped the tools he made, believing that it was through them that he received what little sustenance he had.

Santosh squandered nearly all of his earnings on his drinking habit. His wife and children lived in fear of him, dreading the next time he would come home and beat them.

Two Gospel for Asia missionaries had compassion on Santosh and reached out to him with God's Word, but he scorned them and told them there was no god but Biskarma (tools). One day they invited Santosh to church, and they were surprised to see him sitting in the back the next Sunday.

Santosh was delighted to hear the music in his native tongue, and he slowly joined in, singing and clapping his hands. He welcomed the missionaries in his home each week and began to attend Sunday worship regularly. Santosh continued to hear the teaching of God's Word, received Christ, and was freed from his alcohol addiction.

Santosh now felt a burden for his people. With the missionaries' help, he applied to study at a Bible college so that he would be better equipped to share the gospel with the worshipers of Biskarma.

The villagers responded to Santosh's witness with severe opposition. The day before he was to leave for Bible college, a large group confronted him, threatening to beat him and chase him from the village if he did not return to his traditions. Santosh stood firm, devoted to the God who had redeemed his life from brokenness. The villagers continued to threaten Santosh's family, and eventually his wife and children came to live with him at the campus.

Today, this "Untouchable" lives a life of incredible purpose. Santosh knows that God loves and values him. Because of Santosh's ministry and powerful witness, a new church with active believers worships the true God, who has not forgotten the oppressed Dalits. Santosh and other Dalit believers have come to know the truth that enables them to stand against threats and opposition: Jesus' love is better than life.

Father, before we knew You, we were all Untouchables, broken and impoverished and without hope. Thank You for Your love, which is better than life. May our lips always glorify You.

SOURCE: GOSPEL FOR ASIA

PERSECUTION WATCH: NORTH KOREA

Having one of the most repressive and isolated regimes in the world, the communist nation of North Korea persecutes Christians more severely than any other nation, experts believe. Dictator Kim Jong Il works to eradicate all belief systems and requires that citizens worship only him. The government denies every kind of human right to its citizens.

It is difficult, with this oppressive regime, to know exactly how many Christians there are in North Korea, but stories of their faith and suffering travel along with the refugees who flee across the border into China. Thousands of Christians have been murdered since the Korean War. Voice of the Martyrs reports that in 1953, there were about 300,000 Christians in North Korea; the number has been reduced to a few thousand today, and many of those are suffering in labor camps. Those who have not been detained must practice their faith in deep secrecy and are constantly in danger.

One ministry organization that attempts to provide Bibles

for these suffering Christians shares some of the stories that have made their way back. A man was executed when he was caught with two New Testaments in his possession. A North Korean army general who became a Christian was executed by a fellow officer for trying to share the gospel with some of the people in his unit. A woman who was washing her clothes made the fatal mistake of carrying a New Testament in her pocket. It fell out when she bent over to rinse her laundry—and both she and her grandmother were quickly executed.

Despite all of these efforts to destroy it, the church in North Korea has survived. Christian refugees who escape into China report that there are small house churches, usually including only family members. One possible explanation for the growth of the church is that in the midst of oppression and human injustice, people still seek answers that the government can't give. North Korean Christians have the answer. There is a way to believe that offers true freedom, hope, and justice. Pray that God will grant freedom to His church in North Korea and protect His people there until that time.

SOURCE: MISSION NETWORK NEWS

My Brother's Keeper

Am I my brother's keeper?

GENESIS 4:9

Son Jong Hoon, a South Korean, visited the United States to plead with the world to pressure North Korea to release his elder brother, Son Jong Nam, awaiting public execution for the crime of simply being a Christian.

For more than a year, Nam, former North Korean Army officer turned underground evangelist, has been beaten, tortured, and held in a bleak, North Korean death row basement jail in the capital city. He has been sentenced to public execution as an example to the North Korean people.

"My only purpose in life right now is to save my brother," the younger Son said. "I pray to God for my brother's safety."

Some years ago the elder Son complained to the North Korean Central People's Committee when his pregnant wife, while being investigated by the secret police, was kicked in the stomach and miscarried. He made plans to leave North Korea after being pressured to drop the matter.

Nam defected to China in 1998 with his wife, son, and brother. His wife died after arriving there. It was in China that he met a South Korean missionary and became a Christian. Nam continued his religious studies and felt called to be an evangelist in North Korea.

But before he could return home, Nam was arrested by Chinese police in 2001 and sent back to North Korea, charged with sending missionaries to his native country. He was imprisoned and brutally tortured for three years.

Nam was released on parole in May 2004 and expelled from Pyongyang to Chongjin to work at a rocket research institute. However, his health was so bad when he was released that he was unable to walk. But after receiving medical treatment, he went back to China to meet with his brother.

Nam was arrested again when he returned to North Korea in January 2006 and has remained in prison since. The last word of him came in February 2007. It is suspected that because he is being kept in the capitol city, North Korean officials view him as a special case and perhaps are keeping him alive, if barely, for unknown reasons.

Father, help us to remember that we are our brothers' and sisters' keepers, and give us a desire to do what we can to support Your people who are suffering for You around the globe.

SOURCE: MISSION NETWORK NEWS

Huge waves that would frighten an ordinary swimmer produce a tremendous thrill for the surfer who has ridden them. Let's apply that to our own circumstances. The things we try to avoid and fight against—tribulation, suffering, and persecution—are the very things that produce abundant joy in us. "We are more than conquerors through Him" "*in* all these things"; not in spite of them, but in the midst of them. A saint doesn't know the joy of the Lord in spite of tribulation, but *because* of it. Paul said, "I am exceedingly joyful in all our tribulation" (2 Corinthians 7:4).

The undiminished radiance, which is the result of abundant joy, is not built on anything passing, but on the love of God that nothing can change. And the experiences of life, whether they are everyday events or terrifying ones, are powerless to "separate us from the love of God which is in Christ Jesus our Lord" (Romans 8:39).

OSWALD CHAMBERS, *MY UTMOST FOR HIS HIGHEST*

Pure Joy

*Consider it pure joy, my brothers, whenever you face trials
of many kinds, because you know that the testing of your faith
develops perseverance.*

JAMES 1:2

Luis Seoane learned at a young age that standing for the
gospel sometimes results in difficulties. It is often in
those times of difficulty, though, that we learn the discipline of dependence on God as He molds us into people He
can use for His glory.

Luis was born in Madrid, Spain, to a military family during the dictatorship of General Franco. While Luis's family
had a superficial interest in God and the Bible, "there really
wasn't something we could follow," Luis explains.

When Luis was twelve, his father died after a trying
struggle with cancer. Luis became angry with God and wondered if He really cared for him and his family. At age thirteen, Luis's search for answers led him to a neighborhood

church's Bible study, and after a year, he came to know the Lord and found the peace he was seeking.

Although Luis found peace in this relationship with his heavenly Father, the relationship with his mother was strained. She was not happy that her son was reading the Bible, and she was troubled that he was attending a Protestant Salvation Army church. Many nights Luis heard his mother crying herself to sleep, and he knew that his faith was the cause. Eventually, Luis's mother gave him an ultimatum: either stop reading the Bible and return to the way things were before his conversion or go to a military boarding school in Madrid that was nearly four hundred miles away.

At the same time that Luis encountered resistance for his faith at home, he also faced it publicly as he shared the gospel. Believing that they answered to a higher authority, Luis and his Christian friends would hold illegal preaching services in the streets. Initially the police harassed these young believers, but eventually the relationship became cordial, and Luis had the opportunity to share the gospel with the police officers.

But Luis's mother could never accept his faith, and at age thirteen he was sent to a military boarding school in Madrid, where he was the only Protestant among the 650 students in the school. Both teachers and students ridiculed Luis for his faith, especially when he refused to pray for his father during a prayer service for the dead. But it was in these difficult times of opposition and loneliness that Luis's dedication to God was strengthened, and he became even more committed to let his light shine for Christ.

The trials Luis experienced as a youth prepared him for a life of service, and he now serves as regional director of the RBC Ministries office for the Americas in Brazil. The testing of Luis's faith developed the perseverance that makes him an effective servant for Christ today.

Father, it is so easy for us to resent the trials in our lives and become angry with You in the difficult times. By Your Spirit, remind us that these struggles come from Your hand to develop perseverance so that we can more effectively serve You.

SOURCE: *WORDS TO LIVE BY*

The Fellowship of His Sufferings

I want to know Christ and the power of his resurrection and the
fellowship of sharing in his sufferings, becoming like him in his
death, and so, somehow, to attain to the resurrection from the dead.

PHILIPPIANS 3:10–11

At seventeen, Santino Garang (now called Joseph) had already experienced unimaginable suffering. When he was seven, Joseph watched as murahaleen (Arab slave traders) invaded his southern Sudanese village and slaughtered his family. He and the other village children were kidnapped and sold in the slave markets in the north, and he was given an Arab name.

Joseph's Muslim master Ibrahim was cruel, calling him "Black Slave" and giving him only leftover scraps for food. Ibrahim beat Joseph and mocked him for his Christian faith. African slaves—especially Christians—are perceived as being lower than animals. For ten years, Ibrahim ridiculed Joseph's desire to worship, reminding him that someone who had no more value than a donkey had no business worshiping God.

Joseph was responsible for tending his master's camels and fetching water, and one Sunday morning as he was working, he heard the sound of singing. The sounds revived childhood memories of church services, and he experienced joy as he praised God with the worshipers.

His exhilaration was followed by tragedy when Joseph returned to his master with several camels unaccounted for. Ibrahim flew into a rage and threatened to kill Joseph. He decided the suitable punishment for this slave boy was the same one his Lord had received: crucifixion.

After beating Joseph's head and body, Ibrahim laid him out on a plank. He drove nine-inch nails through Joseph's hands, knees, and feet and then poured acid over his legs to increase his pain. Then Ibrahim left Joseph for dead.

Joseph survived because Ibrahim's son heard his cries for help and took pity on him. At great risk to himself, he brought food and water to Joseph for about a week and eventually pulled out the nails and took him to a medical clinic.

Somehow Joseph survived, but he was permanently crippled from his wounds, so Ibrahim had no use for him.

Christians redeemed Joseph and arranged for him to return home, where he was warmly welcomed by the village elders and given the name Joseph. Like Joseph in the Old Testament, this boy had been sold into slavery.

Ibrahim suffered no consequences for his crime. Under Islamic Sharia law, he was acting within his rights.

Unlike the biblical Joseph, however, this Joseph enjoyed no happy reunion with his family and no prosperity. He suffers physical and emotional pain from the loss of his parents, his kidnapping and enslavement, and his nearly fatal ordeal. He is one of a small number of twenty-first-century Christians who know what it means to share in the crucifixion sufferings of Jesus.

Lord, our hearts ache for Your people around the world who are sharing in Your sufferings. As they suffer like You in their pain and even deaths, comfort them with the hope of the resurrection they will share as well.

SOURCE: PERSECUTION PROJECT FOUNDATION

THESE SCARS

I was taken
Just a young child
Bound and marked for slavery
So forsaken
Stripped of all life
Could this be my destiny?

But Lord, You sent someone to find me
And though I leave that place behind me

These scars
Remind me of the love You have for me
Were it not for You, where would I be?
For these scars
Point me to the cross of Calvary
I bear them in Your name
And I won't be ashamed
Of these scars
What can man do

But take the body
Death has lost its grip on me
With Your blood You
Claimed and bought me
You have set my spirit free

And Lord, with every pain I'm yearning
To know the suffering of Your journey

Let these marks I bear
Tell of more than loss
Point them to Your cross, Lord
I will boldly wear
These marks that tell the world
Jesus, I am Yours

SHANNON J. WEXELBERG,
FROM THE CD *BETTER THAN LIFE*

These Scars

I bear on my body the marks of Jesus.

GALATIANS 6:17

The Trokosi slaves of Ghana live as human sacrifices, victims of ritual servitude who are sold into bondage to meet the demands of the fetish priests who serve the idol gods of the shrines. Just prior to their adolescence, young girls are forced into this life of slavery, often to atone for a family member's wrongdoing or to break a curse. Trokosi (meaning "wives of the gods") slave girls work long hours without pay, live with constant hunger, and serve the shrine priest sexually. They are shown no affection, and over time, they bear, on average, four children to the priest who repeatedly rapes them. Fetish priests often carve the faces of these "wives of the gods" to humiliate them and remind them of their bondage.

Organizations like Every Child Ministries (ECM) and

I. N. Network have been successful in raising money to free these children from their oppressors. Liberating these young girls from immense suffering is only the first step; the task then becomes freeing them from spiritual and emotional bondage and helping them rebuild their broken lives. ECM offers these girls the opportunity to know Jesus, and many of them experience the complete freedom of His love and forgiveness.

"Esther" was one of those former Trokosi who came to know Jesus. Once liberated, she returned to school and completed her education.

Even in her new life, though, Esther bore the visible evidence of her past. The scars that still marked her brought continued humiliation as other students refused to associate with her, fearing that they might be invoking some kind of curse upon themselves. Esther asked ECM if the organization could help her find a way to get the scars removed.

When Esther began helping other girls trapped in slavery, however, she began to realize that her scars were a "visual aid." Trokosi were told, "Once you have been a shrine slave, you can never be a Christian. You will die. You will go mad." But as these slave girls encountered Esther, a former shrine slave with all of her scars, telling them about Jesus, they saw living proof that they could receive Christ, just as Esther had. And through Esther's ministry as a Bible teacher and counselor working with ECM, many have.

Esther realizes now that her scars serve a higher purpose: they point others to the cross of Christ and show the world that she belongs to Him. She has come to peace with these scars, she says, and she no longer wants ECM to find a way to have them removed.

Father, in the scars of our lives, may others see the healing that only Jesus can give. Please use our scars, not as a reminder of loss, but as signs pointing others to the freedom we have in His cross.

SOURCE: I.N. NETWORK

The Greatest of These

Love is kind . . . It always protects, always trusts,
always hopes, always perseveres . . . These three remain: faith, hope
and love. But the greatest of these is love.

1 CORINTHIANS 13:4, 7, 13

Often sentences that include the name of missionary Graham Stains also include the word *love*. Graham's love for God and his compassion for leprosy victims brought him to Baripada, India, in 1983, where he oversaw the work of the Leprosy Home, serving the patients there. Australian born Stains loved his wife Gladys, who worked with him, and his children, Esther, Philip, and Timothy. He loved the gospel, and he shared it faithfully. And he loved the people of Manoharpur, the place where he last ministered to people in the remote hills of India—where he and his two young sons were burned alive for their faith in Jesus Christ.

In January 1999, Graham and his sons traveled to the village of Manoharpur to conduct an annual "jungle camp," where he would provide Bible teaching and training in health and hygiene. He had been conducting the camp for fourteen years, and the families who lived there looked forward to his visit. The trip was a challenge in many ways—Graham and his sons, ages ten and eight, traveled across ravines and through unfriendly terrain to reach this village in the hills where there was no electricity and no running water.

Graham knew that the tribal Hindus of the area strongly opposed the Christians in the state of Orissa, where Manoharpur was located. There had been at least sixty attacks on churches in Orissa between 1986 and 1998. He was also aware that this tension had reached the village where he was holding the jungle camp. And yet he went with his two sons, realizing that the personal cost for his commitment to Christ could be great.

Because the weather was cold, Graham and the boys were sleeping in the family station wagon, which was parked near the church where they had been ministering.

Around 12:30 in the morning, a mob of about fifty people approached the station wagon, screaming and swinging axes and other weapons. The attackers broke the windows of the vehicle and prevented the Stains from escaping. They beat the three mercilessly, put straw under the station wagon, and then torched it. They blocked the doors to the village huts and surrounded the vehicle so that no one would be able to help.

After the mob left and all that remained was the burned-out shell of the station wagon, the bodies of Graham, Philip, and Timothy, charred beyond recognition, yet locked in an embrace, were all that was left.

Gladys and Esther continued to live in India until 2004, when they returned to Australia so that Esther could attend medical school. Until that time, Gladys continued Graham's work and oversaw the completion of a hospital for leprosy patients in Baripada; the Graham Stains Memorial Hospital opened July 8, 2004. In 2005, Gladys received India's Padma Shri award for distinguished service, an award that is the equivalent of being knighted in England. Both Gladys and Esther thank God that He considered Graham, Philip, and Timothy worthy to die for Him.

Father, may love always motivate us, even when the world hates us. Keep us in that "most excellent way," so that what we do—in love—endures.

SOURCE: MISSION NETWORK NEWS

Not Abandoned

We are hard pressed on every side, but not crushed; perplexed, but not in despair; persecuted, but not abandoned; struck down, but not destroyed ... For our light and momentary troubles are achieving for us an eternal glory that far outweighs them all.

2 CORINTHIANS 4:8–9, 17

As recently as January 2007, China received International Christian Concern's Hall of Shame award as one of the world's top ten nations persecuting Christians. Some Christians in China risk their lives daily, their only crime being faith in Christ. In a country where the only legal churches are those controlled by China's atheistic government, more Christians are imprisoned than in any other nation in the world.

A victim of the Chinese government's opposition to the gospel, Pastor Cai Zhuohua currently serves a three-year prison sentence. As Pastor Cai waited for a bus in Beijing on September 11, 2004, he was arrested and dragged into a van by state security officers. None of his family members were officially notified of his arrest, and Pastor Cai was tortured with electric cattle prods until he was forced to confess. Over a year later, in November 2005, Pastor Cai was found guilty of "illegal business practices" for playing a key role in the printing and distribution of Bibles and other Christian literature, even though these materials were given away rather than sold for profit, and his activities were not illegal.

Reports from two of the prisons where Pastor Cai has been incarcerated are bleak. In Tianhe Prison, he was forced to work more than ten hours a day making handbags, and in Qianjin Prison, where Pastor Cai was transferred in April 2006, prisoners are not allowed to speak during work and must ask permission to use the toilet. The heavy work is physically demanding, and there are reports that Pastor Cai's health is deteriorating because of the poor quality of the prison food.

Pastor Cai's wife, her brother, and her brother's wife were tried on the same charges. Their arrests came a few weeks after Pastor Cai's, and they were tortured into making confessions as well. Xiao Yunfei, Cai's wife, was found guilty and sentenced to two years in prison, and her brother was sentenced to eighteen months. Her brother's wife was released. Cai's mother cares for his young son while Cai and Xiao are in prison.

Even those who attempted to help Pastor Cai with his legal battles have suffered. Gao Zhisheng, a human rights attorney on Cai's defense team, received notice shortly before Cai's sentencing that he had to suspend his law practice for a year, making it nearly impossible for his firm to file an appeal within the required time frame.

Yet God has not abandoned His church in China. The church continues to grow, and while it is difficult to come up with an official number, some estimates say there are nearly forty million Christians in China, with millions in remote areas and millions more attending the nation's unregistered house churches.

Heavenly Father, comfort Your people in China with the truth that You have not abandoned them. Provide physical and spiritual strength for the thousands who have been imprisoned for their faith in You, and give boldness to Chinese Christians to share the gospel, even though they face great danger.

SOURCE: VOICE OF THE MARTYRS

STAND UP, STAND UP FOR JESUS

Stand up, stand up for Jesus,
Ye soldiers of the cross;
Lift high His royal banner,
It must not suffer loss:
From vict'ry unto vict'ry
His army shall He lead,
Till ev'ry foe is vanquished,
And Christ is Lord indeed.

Stand up, stand up for Jesus,
The strife will not be long;
This day the noise of battle,
The next the victor's song:
To Him that overcometh,
A crown of life shall be:
He with the King of glory
Shall reign eternally.

GEORGE DUFFIELD, JR.

PERSECUTION WATCH: ERITREA

Sandwiched between the Sudan and Ethiopia and bordered on the east by the Red Sea, Eritrea is a small African nation that has struggled to acquire and maintain its independence. Growing tensions with both Ethiopia and the Sudan make the government of this small nation suspicious of anything that would distract its citizens from offering their highest allegiance to their country, and the government's determination to maintain control internally has resulted in viewing anyone who does not follow a certain standard as an enemy of the state.

Even though the United States includes Eritrea on its list of nations with the worst human rights offenses, Eritrean officials would insist that its citizens have the freedom to practice religion. But in 2002, the government began a registration system for religions, and religious groups were forced to submit information about themselves in order to hold worship services. The only religions or denominations that have been recognized are Islam, Catholicism, and Orthodox. And since that time, government authorities have been arresting members of minority denominations, or, as officials call them, "new religions."

Recent reports suggest that one out of every ten Christians in Eritrea is persecuted for their faith. About two thousand Christians are imprisoned in horrible conditions, and there are reports of those who have been locked up in metal shipping containers without ventilation or bathroom facilities. Christians are detained, tortured, and sometimes executed without ever being brought before a court of law to be formally charged or tried.

In February of 2005, Mission Network News reported that police in Asmara, the capital city, arrested 131 Christian children between the ages of two and eighteen. They took the children from their classes to the police station to register their names and addresses.

While the children were at the police station, they began singing in loud voices, "I am not afraid of persecution, hardships, and even death. Nobody can separate me from the love of Jesus Christ. He died on the cross, and He gave me new life."

The children continued to sing, even when the policemen threatened them. When the police turned on a television to drown out their songs, the children protested. The police responded by beating them.

The children were detained at the police station for nearly four hours. Those younger than fifteen were eventually released and told to return the next week with their parents. At least thirty of the children, older teenagers, remained in custody and were transferred to another police station. At a young age, these children are learning the cost of praising Jesus.

In another reported case, two young Christian men were tortured to death in 2006. Immanuel Andegergesh, 23, and Kibrom Firemichel, 30, died while in custody, just two days after they were arrested at a religious service in a private home south of Asmara.

In 2007, the death of Magos Solomon Semere, age 30, was reported. He had been jailed four and a half years earlier for worshiping in a banned Protestant church. During his imprisonment, Semere was barred from seeing his fiancé, and he was repeatedly offered medical treatment or release if he would recant his faith. He died in a military jail; he had pneumonia and had been brutally treated by the military authorities there. His former fellow prisoner remarked, "Magos was determined to obey the Lord rather than men."

These cases are just a representation of the thousands who are suffering and dying for the sake of Christ in Eritrea. Pray that God would give Eritrean Christians grace to endure this severe persecution and that they will remain strong in their faith. Pray that the government will be moved to stand by its official May 2003 statement: "No groups or persons are persecuted in Eritrea for their beliefs or religion."

SOURCE: MISSION NETWORK NEWS

Singing in the Shadow

Because you are my help, I sing in the shadow of your wings.

PSALM 63:7

Among the two thousand detained members of banned evangelical churches in Eritrea was Helen Berhane, a gospel singer especially popular with young people. She was released from captivity in October 2006 after being arrested in May 2004 for refusing to recant her faith and cease participating in Christian activities. She had released an album of Christian music just before her arrest.

Even though Helen was never officially charged or put on trial, she was jailed at the Mai Serwa Military Camp. Reportedly, she was tortured many times to get her to recant during her nearly two-year ordeal. Upon her detainment, one military commander told her that she would not be allowed visitors and that she would "rot here until you sign this paper" recanting her faith.

She spent much of her imprisonment in a metal shipping

container that was used as a prison cell, where she was sub-
jected to extreme temperatures in the desert climate. After
a guard caught her listening to a Christian radio program in
her cell, she was imprisoned in an underground cell, where
she was chained for two weeks.

After suffering these inhuman and degrading conditions,
Helen was hospitalized in Asmara, Eritrea's capital city, in
early October 2006 for injuries suffered from new beatings.
Although no reasons were given, officials released Helen later that month, and she remained in a wheelchair for some
time afterwards because of severe injuries to her legs and
feet inflicted by her captors. Helen has not been able to talk
about her experiences since her release; local Christians believe that she probably has been ordered not to talk about
her imprisonment.

Although the Eritrean Constitution guarantees freedom
of religion for all citizens, many, like Helen, suffer for their
religious beliefs and are tortured and pressured to recant or
remain in prison. Their God is their help.

*Our God, many governments seek to destroy the lives of those who
love You. Please comfort those who suffer for Your name's sake in these*

nations. Restore justice so that Your people are no longer persecuted for believing in You.

SOURCE: COMPASS DIRECT NEWS

Now Stephen, a man full of God's grace and power, did great wonders and miraculous signs among the people. Opposition arose, however, from members of the Synagogue of the Freedmen (as it was called)—Jews of Cyrene and Alexandria as well as the provinces of Cilicia and Asia. These men began to argue with Stephen, but they could not stand up against his wisdom or the Spirit by whom he spoke.

Then they secretly persuaded some men to say, "We have heard Stephen speak words of blasphemy against Moses and against God."

So they stirred up the people and the elders and the teachers of the law. They seized Stephen and brought him before the Sanhedrin. They produced false witnesses, who testified, "This fellow never stops speaking against this holy place and against the law. For we have heard him say that this Jesus of Nazareth will destroy this place and change the customs Moses handed down to us."

All who were sitting in the Sanhedrin looked intently at

Stephen, and they saw that his face was like the face of an angel . . .

When [the Sanhedrin] heard [Stephen's testimony], they were furious and gnashed their teeth at him. But Stephen, full of the Holy Spirit, looked up to heaven and saw the glory of God, and Jesus standing at the right hand of God. "Look," he said, "I see heaven open and the Son of Man standing at the right hand of God."

At this they covered their ears and, yelling at the top of their voices, they all rushed at him, dragged him out of the city and began to stone him. Meanwhile, the witnesses laid their clothes at the feet of a young man named Saul.

While they were stoning him, Stephen prayed, "Lord Jesus, receive my spirit."

ACTS 6:8–15; 7:54–59

Rich in Heaven

Blessed are you when people insult you, persecute you and falsely say all kinds of evil against you because of me. Rejoice and be glad, because great is your reward in heaven.

MATTHEW 5:11–12

The leaders of Hopegivers International in Kota, Rajasthan, India, understand what it means to be persecuted because of righteousness. Hindu extremists, who want to end India's secular government and make it a Hindu state, have been running a campaign of terror against Bishop M. A. Thomas, founder, and his son, Dr. Samuel Thomas, president. Hopegivers offers protection to abandoned and orphaned children and education and medical services to the desperately poor through its hospital, orphanages, and schools in Kota.

In February 2006 radical Hindus falsely accused Hopegivers of publishing a book that was critical of two Hindu deities. They arrested members of the Hopegivers' national staff and offered bounties for the heads of Bishop M. A. and Dr. Samuel Thomas, who went into hiding. Eventually, Dr. Samuel was arrested and imprisoned in March of 2006 and was released on bail after forty-seven days.

In the meantime, Rajasthan authorities suspended the licenses of Hopegivers' ministries, including the hospital, orphanages, and schools. They seized the organization's bank accounts. The government of Rajasthan proposed that the 2,500 orphanage children be returned to the streets that they were rescued from.

During the ordeal, Dr. Samuel experienced God's hand of protection. The men who arrested him were armed with guns, and when one of the arresting officers attempted to kill him in the encounter, the gun's trigger locked up. Before he was imprisoned, Dr. Samuel evaded lynching several times. Once in prison, he was kept awake for fourteen days and nights, and his three by six-foot cell was rat infested.

Dr. Samuel has used this oppression, however, to be a steadfast witness for Christ. He and other Hopegivers staff members used their metal eating utensils as drums and sang songs of rejoicing to the Lord. On one occasion, when Dr. Samuel was traveling to court for a hearing, he discovered that the mass murderer who was traveling with him had been sent to kill him on the way. After listening to Dr. Samuel's stories, the assassin, with tears in his eyes, asked for five hundred New Testaments for the people in his cell. As a result of Dr. Samuel's testimony in this situation, people did come to Christ.

As recently as the spring of 2007, both Bishop Thomas and Dr. Samuel were still facing legal battles to clear their names and continue to raise funds to fix the damage that placed their ministry in a financial crisis. Dr. Samuel remains committed to the children of India: "For them, I want to do as much as I can. God has met my needs so I will help the ones who have nothing. I don't want to die rich. I'm already rich in heaven. I want to die doing what I can for others."

Father, thank You for the example of these believers who are willing to die in order to help others. Thank You for preserving their lives so that they can continue to do Your work. Help them to rejoice as they remember the reward that awaits them in heaven.

SOURCE: MISSION NETWORK NEWS

The Crown of Life

To the angel of the church in Smyrna write:
Do not be afraid of what you are about to suffer. I tell you, the
devil will put some of you in prison to test you, and you will suffer
persecution for ten days. Be faithful, even to the point of death,
and I will give you the crown of life.

REVELATION 2:8, 10

On April 18, 2007, five Muslims entered a Christian
publishing company in Turkey and killed three believers in
the southeastern province of Malatya. Two of the victims
were Turkish converts from Islam and the third man was a
German citizen who had lived in Turkey for ten years. News
reports said four of the attackers admitted that the killings
were motivated by both "nationalist and religious feelings."

The following is a letter received by the Voice of the Martyrs
from a church in Turkey.

A Letter to the Global Church from
The Protestant Church of Smyrna

This past week has been filled with much sorrow. Many of you have heard by now of our devastating loss here in an event that took place in Malatya, a Turkish province three hundred miles northeast of Antioch, the city where believers were first called Christians (Acts 11:26).

On Wednesday morning, April 18, 2007, 46-year-old German Christian and father of three Tilmann Geske prepared to go to his office, kissing his wife goodbye and taking a moment to hug his son and give him the priceless memory, "Goodbye, son. I love you."

Tilmann rented an office space from Zirve Publishing. Zirve was also the location of the Malatya Evangelist Church office. A ministry of the church, Zirve prints and distributes Christian literature to Malatya and nearby cities in eastern Turkey. In another area of town, 35-year-old Pastor Necati Aydin, father of two, said goodbye to his wife, leaving for the office as well. Tilmann and Necati had a morning Bible study and prayer meeting that some other believers in town would also be attending. Ugur Yuksel, another Turkish

Zirve worker who was a Christian convert from Islam, like-wise made his way to the Bible study.

Meanwhile, on the other side of town, ten young men all under 20 years of age put into place final arrangements for their ultimate act of faith, living out their love for Allah and hatred of infidels who they felt undermined Islam.

On Resurrection Sunday, five of these men had been to a by-invitation-only evangelistic service that Pastor Necati and his men had arranged at a hotel conference room in the city. The five men were known to the believers as "seekers." No one knows what happened in the hearts of those men as they listened to the gospel. Today we have only the beginning of their story.

These young men, one of whom is the son of a mayor in the province of Malatya, are part of a tarikat, or a group of "faithful believers" in Islam. Tarikat membership is highly respected here; it's like a fraternity membership. In fact, it is said that no one can get into public office without membership in a tarikat. These young men all lived in the same dorm, all preparing for university entrance exams.

The young men got guns, bread knives, ropes, and towels ready for their final act of service to Allah. They knew there would be a lot of blood. They arrived in time for the Bible study, around 10 o'clock.

They arrived, and apparently the Bible study began. Reportedly, after Necati read a chapter from the Bible, the assault began. The boys tied Ugur, Necati, and Tilmann's hands and feet to chairs, and as they videoed their work on their cell phones, they brutally tortured our brothers for almost three hours.

Neighbors in workplaces near the print house said later they had heard yelling, but assumed the owners were having a domestic argument so they did not respond.

Meanwhile, another believer, Gokhan, and his wife had a leisurely morning. He slept in till 10, ate a long breakfast, and finally around 12:30 he and his wife arrived at the office. The door was locked from the inside, and his key would not work. He phoned, and though it had connection on his end, he did not hear the phone ringing inside. He called the cell phones of his brothers, and finally Ugur answered his phone. "We are not at the office. Go to the hotel meeting. We are there. We will come there," he said cryptically. As Ugur spoke, Gokhan heard in the telephone's background weeping and a strange snarling sound.

He phoned the police, and the nearest officer arrived in about five minutes. He pounded on the door, "Police, open up!" Initially the officer thought it was a domestic disturbance. At that point they heard another snarl and a gurgling moan. The policeman understood that sound as human suffering, prepared the clip in his gun and tried over and over again to burst through the door. One of the frightened assailants unlocked the door for the policeman, who entered to find a grisly scene.

Tilmann and Necati had been slaughtered. Ugur's throat was likewise slit and he was barely alive.

Three assailants in front of the policeman dropped their weapons.

Meanwhile Gokhan heard the sound of yelling in the street. Someone had fallen from their third-story office. Running down, he found a man on the ground, whom he later recognized, named Emre Gunaydin. He had massive head trauma and, strangely, was snarling. He had tried to climb down the drainpipe to escape, and, losing his balance, had plummeted to the ground. It seems that he was the main leader of the attackers. Another assailant was found hiding on a lower balcony.

To untangle the web we need to back up six years. In

April 2001, the National Security Council of Turkey (Milli Guvenlik Kurulu) began to consider evangelical Christians to be a threat to national security, on equal footing with Al Qaeda and PKK terrorism. Statements made in the press by political leaders, columnists, and commentators have fueled a hatred against "missionaries," who they claim bribe young people to change their religion.

After that decision in 2001, attacks and threats on churches, pastors, and Christians began. Bombings, physical attacks, verbal and written abuse are only some of the ways Christians are being targeted. Most significant is the use of media propaganda . . .

In an official televised response from Ankara, the interior minister of Turkey smirked as he spoke of the attacks on our brothers in Malatya. Amid public outrage and protests against the event and in favor of freedom of religion and freedom of thought, media and official comments ring with the same message, "We hope you have learned your lesson. We do not want Christians here." . . .

The young men involved in the killing are currently in custody. Today's news reported that they would be tried as terrorists, so their age would not affect the strict penalty. Assailant Emre Gunaydin is still in intensive care. The investigation centers around him and his contacts, and they say the case will fall apart if he does not recover.

The church in Turkey responded in a way that honored God as dozens of believers and pastors flew in as fast as they could to stand by the small church of Malatya and encourage the believers, take care of legal issues, and represent Christians to the media.

When Susanne [Geske] expressed her wish to bury her husband in Malatya, the governor tried to stop it, and when he realized he could not stop it, a rumor was spread that "it is a sin to dig a grave for a Christian." In the end, in an undertaking that should be remembered in Christian history forever, the men from the church in Adana (near Tarsus), grabbed shovels and dug a grave for their slain brother in an untended hundred-year-old Armenian graveyard.

Ugur was buried by his family in an Alevi Muslim ceremony in his hometown of Elazig, his believing fiancé watching from the shadows as his family and friends refused to accept in death the faith Ugur had so long professed and died for.

Necati's funeral took place in his hometown of Izmir, the city where he came to faith. The darkness does not understand the light. Though the churches expressed their forgiveness for the event, Christians were not to be trusted.

Before workers would load the coffin onto the plane from Malatya, it went through two separate X-ray exams to make sure it was not loaded with explosives. This is not a usual procedure for Muslim coffins.

Necati's funeral was a beautiful event. Like a glimpse of heaven, hundreds of Turkish Christians and workers came to show their love for Christ and their honor for this man chosen to die for Christ. Necati's wife Shemsa told the world, "His death was full of meaning, because he died for Christ and he lived for Christ . . . Necati was a gift from God. I feel honored that he was in my life, I feel crowned with honor. I want to be worthy of that honor."

Boldly the believers took their stand at Necati's funeral, facing the risks of being seen publicly and likewise becoming targets. As expected, the anti-terror police attended and videotaped everyone attending the funeral for their future use. The service took place outside at Buca Baptist Church, and he was buried in a small Christian graveyard in the outskirts of Izmir.

Two assistant governors of Izmir were there solemnly watching the event from the front row. Dozens of news agencies were there documenting the events with live news and photographs. Who knows the impact the funeral had on those watching? This is the beginning of their story as well. Pray for them.

In an act that hit front pages in the largest newspapers in Turkey, Susanne Geske in a television interview expressed her forgiveness. She did not want revenge, she told reporters. "Oh God, forgive them for they know not what they do," she said, wholeheartedly agreeing with the words of Christ on Calvary (Luke 23:34).

In a country where blood-for-blood revenge is as normal as breathing, many, many reports have come to the attention of the church of how this comment of Susanne Geske has changed lives. One columnist wrote of her comment, "She said in one sentence what 1000 missionaries in 1000 years could never do."

Many foreigners in Malatya will most likely move out, as their families and children have become publicly identified as targets to the hostile city. The remaining ten believers are in hiding. What will happen to this church, this light in the darkness? Most likely it will go underground. Pray for wisdom, that Turkish brothers from other cities will go to lead the leaderless church. Should we not be concerned for that great city of Malatya, a city that does not know what it is doing? (Jonah 4:11).

When our pastor, Fikret Bocek, went with a brother to give a statement to the Security Directorate on Monday, they were ushered into the Anti-Terror Department. On the wall was a huge chart covering the whole wall listing all the terrorist cells in Izmir, categorized. In one prominent column were listed all the evangelical churches in Izmir. The darkness does not understand the light. "These that have turned the world upside down are come hither also" (Acts 17:6).

Please pray for the church in Turkey. "Don't pray against persecution, pray for perseverance," urges Pastor Fikret Bocek.

The church is better having lost our brothers; the fruit in our lives, the renewed faith, the burning desire to spread the gospel to quench more darkness in Malatya . . . all these are not to be regretted. Pray that we stand strong against external opposition and especially pray that we stand strong against internal struggles with sin, our true debilitating weakness.

This we know. Christ Jesus was there when our brothers were giving their lives for Him. He was there, like He was when Stephen was being stoned in the sight of Saul of Tarsus.

Someday the video of the deaths of our brothers may reveal more to us about the strength that we know Christ gave them to endure their last cross, about the peace the Spirit of

God endowed them with to suffer for their beloved Savior. But we know He did not leave their side. We know their minds were full of Scripture strengthening them to endure, as darkness tried to subdue the unsubduable Light of the Gospel. We know, in whatever way they were able, with a look or a word, they encouraged one another to stand strong. We know they knew they would soon be with Christ.

We don't know the details. We don't know the kind of justice that will or will not be served on this earth.

But we pray—and urge you to pray—that someday at least one of those five boys will come to faith because of the testimony in death of Tilmann Geske, who gave his life as a foreign Christian in Turkey, and the testimonies in death of Necati Aydin and Ugur Yuksel, the first martyrs for Christ out of the Turkish church.

Details in this letter were obtained through various news and media sources based on preliminary press releases and interviews. The court cases are pending and specific evidence and autopsy reports from the crime are not yet available to the public.

REPORTED BY DARLENE N. BOCEK, 01 MAY 2007

Eric Liddell was the Olympic champion whose story was made famous in the movie Chariots of Fire. *Later in life, he served as a missionary to China and died while he was imprisoned in a WWII Japanese internment camp in 1945.*

When Eric [Liddell] spoke in church or led a Bible study group with [his fellow prisoners], he rarely dealt with what might happen tomorrow. Instead, he focused on what could happen today. During one small group discussion, he read aloud the words of Jesus in Matthew 5:43: "Love your enemies, bless them that curse you, do good to them that hate you, and pray for them which despitefully use you, and persecute you." Then he asked if this was merely an ideal or something practical they could actually do. Could they love the guards in camp and the Japanese people as a whole? Most thought it was only a lofty goal.

"I thought so too," Eric said, "but then I noticed the next words, 'Pray for them that despitefully use you.' When we start to pray," he said, "we become God-centered. When we hate then we're self-centered. We spend a lot of time praying for people we like but we don't spend much time praying for people we don't like and people we hate. But Jesus told us to pray for our enemies. I've begun to pray for the guards and it's changed my whole attitude toward them. Maybe you'd like to try it too."

FROM *ERIC LIDDELL: PURE GOLD* BY DAVID MCCASLAND

Your Thoughts for Me

All the days ordained for me were written in your book before one of them came to be. How precious to me are your thoughts, O God! How vast is the sum of them!

PSALM 139:16–17

Persecution takes many forms, and sometimes it comes from the hands of those we would expect to be our protectors—our families. Monique Govender, an RBC Ministries staff member in the Pretoria, South Africa, office found the greatest opposition to her fledgling faith in her own home.

Monique grew up in Durban, South Africa, in a large, poor family in a strict Hindu home. Idol worship was a part of everyday life, and the family was careful to observe Hindu customs and pray the required prayers to many gods. Tragedy came to her family when two of her siblings died in the space of twenty days. While the family remained Hindu, her mother feared that she might lose all of her children and began praying secretly in a Christian church on her way to work every day. In the meantime, Monique's father hated Christians, and his hatred seemed to be motivated by some misunderstandings he had about Christianity.

During her childhood, Monique was introduced to Christianity at several different points, and each time the experience made an impression. As a four-year-old, she attended a memorable church activity; on an errand to buy alcohol for her father one day, Monique, then seven, saw two skits—one about the ten virgins and one about Joseph; and the greatest influence of all was finding out that her grandparents had become Christians and then attending church with them one Sunday morning.

Her family in crisis because of her father's alcoholism and abusive behavior, Monique became a Christian at the age of fifteen at the urging of a zealous school classmate. Her brother had become a Christian as well when someone gave him a Bible to read, and Monique observed significant changes in his life.

Monique's father was unhappy to see two of his children turning to Christ, and he became even more abusive, especially toward his son. Monique was forbidden to attend church, and even though she was an inexperienced young

Christian and didn't own a Bible, she turned to prayer. Eventually, she was allowed to go to church, and in time both her parents came to know Christ as well.

In spite of the obstacles—growing up in a Hindu home with a father who opposed her Christianity—Monique's faith has flourished. She reflects on her past: "I am not sure of what God's thoughts were for me, but in looking back, it seems like He's been thinking about me. And it's just marvelous to me to think that I was just an unknown girl . . . God knew me, and even as a little child, I could feel that God was there with me."

God, You have ordained each of our days and have created us to be vessels to serve You, wherever You have placed us, in whatever difficulties we may face. We do not understand Your thoughts, but we know that You are mindful of us, and we thank You that You are always with us, providing what we need to overcome the opposition to our faith.

SOURCE: *WORDS TO LIVE BY*

PERSECUTION WATCH: CHINA

In 1949, the People's Republic of China was formed under Chairman Mao Zedong. He quickly began purging the country of anything that did not coincide with his vision of a communist nation, resulting in millions of deaths.

In recent years there has been a move to a free market economy. However, that freedom has not carried over into human rights and religious freedom.

China's human rights record is one of the worst in the world, with a system of "re-education through labor" that detains hundreds of thousands each year in work camps without even a court hearing. There are more Christians in prison in China than in any other country in the world. The only legal churches are those strictly controlled by the government. Those who do not wish to follow government policies on religious practice and beliefs must meet in homes and risk being labeled evil cults. Such a designation can result in closing down the church, confiscation of property, and charges against the leadership, often resulting in torture, imprisonment, and death.

In November 2004, the Chinese government announced a new set of regulations to govern religious affairs. While the government claimed that these regulations would bring about significant steps toward religious freedom, it appears that they served only to codify policies in various existing laws.

Ironically, it was during that same month that China Aid was able to obtain a document that had been issued on May 27, 2004, outlining the government's agenda to "boost Marxist atheism research, propaganda, and education." One intention was to "ban all uncivilized conduct in spreading superstitions," causing citizens to be "educated, [have their] spirits enriched, their state of thought improved." The government urged stronger media involvement, with a focus on the Internet as "a new tool to conduct Marxist atheism propaganda and education." While the document was purported to support freedom of religion, it called on officials to make a distinction between religion and "superstition." The "superstition" designation has been frequently used against religious beliefs that do not support the government's Marxist position. This document became the basis to justify increased government suppression of house churches, the Internet, and Christian literature.

A second official Chinese government document outlined a new offensive on underground house churches. In part, the document reads: "We must resolutely and strongly deal with the unregistered house churches. They are too numerous—too many. We must deal with them strongly." The document suggests the increased pressure would be from April to August 2005. It was reported that on May 22, 2005, during Sunday worship time, police and Public Security Bureau (PSB) officers simultaneously raided approximately sixty house churches in Changchun, the capital city of Jilin province in northeastern China. In the days following, an additional forty churches in the area were also raided. More than six hundred house church believers and leaders were taken into custody. Most were released after twenty-four to forty-eight hours of interrogation, but approximately one hundred leaders continued to be held in different detention centers.

During 2004, several mass arrests clarified the government's objectives regarding house churches. In a single raid on a leadership retreat on June 11, 2004, police arrested more than one hundred leaders of the China Gospel Fellowship (CGF) house church movement. Chinese authorities also raided a leadership retreat on July 12, 2004, arresting over one hundred church leaders. Then, for the third time in two months, Chinese authorities rounded up large numbers of house church leaders as they gathered together for mutual encouragement and fellowship in August 2004.

There has been no respite from individual arrests, imprisonment, and torture. On June 18, 2004, Ms. Jiang Zongxiu was beaten to death while in prison. Despite reports in the Chinese media and several appeals to higher authorities, there was no serious investigation into the case. Initially, the authorities claimed she had died of heart failure, despite the obvious wounds on her body from the beatings.

Another prominent house church pastor, Zhang Rongliang, was arrested on December 1, 2004. Rongliang had been denied travel documents and was arrested because he obtained illegal documents to be able to leave the country to attend a mission conference. He was sentenced to seven-and-a-half years in prison. The sentence was particularly harsh because Rongliang had been in prison five times before for a total of twelve years. Currently, his health is failing in prison, as he suffers from high blood pressure, severe diabetes, and arthritis. His sons, in ministry also, are in hiding, and his wife is permitted to visit him only once a month. Because of Rongliang's witness in his prison cell and in neighboring cells, forty to fifty people have become Christians.

These are only two of the thousands of Christians risking their lives daily in China. Their only crime is faith in Jesus Christ. Thankfully, the government has been responsive at times to international pressure. However, this responsiveness is sporadic, and too frequently Western governments have been more obsessed with gaining access into the huge Chinese market than to require basic human rights for the people.

Despite the opposition, the church in China is growing rapidly, something the government is fighting hard to contain. Pray for spiritual and physical strength for the thousands of Christians in prison for their faith in China.

SOURCES: VOICE OF THE MARTYRS, CANADA; MISSION NETWORK NEWS

The Cost of Remembering

Remember those in prison as if you were their fellow prisoners, and those who are mistreated as if you yourselves were suffering.

HEBREWS 13:3

Remembering fellow believers and their suffering and mistreatment sometimes can be costly, as Liu Fenggang, a Chinese Christian from Beijing, can testify. A member of China's unofficial house church, Liu is committed to providing support for persecuted Christians. His reports about persecuted Christians in China have been published in the United States and other overseas countries, but it was his investigation of and reporting on the persecution of Christians in Zhejiang that brought about his own arrest and imprisonment.

In March 2003, Chinese authorities began cracking down on underground churches and began demolishing Protestant, Catholic, and Buddhist houses of worship. Police arrested more than three hundred members of house churches in Zhejiang, beating and imprisoning them. When Liu learned of this situation, he went to Zhejiang to investigate and write about what he learned.

It was not surprising, then, that Liu himself was arrested on October 13, 2003. Under the Chinese legal system, a prisoner can be held for months before being formally charged or brought to trial. Finally on August 6, 2004, Liu was sentenced to three years' imprisonment for "secretly gathering and illegally providing state intelligence to organizations outside the country."

This was not Liu's first experience with prison. His commitment to religious freedom and protecting the rights of persecuted Christians has resulted in frequent house arrests and harsh beatings. Prior to this imprisonment, he spent three years in a labor camp. During his labor camp imprisonment, which began in 1995, his mother died and his infant son grew up without him.

During this most recent imprisonment, Liu was hospitalized five times because he was not receiving proper treatment for his heart condition and diabetes.

Liu was released from prison and returned to his home in Beijing on February 5, 2007. He underwent successful heart surgery at the end of February. But Chinese authorities con-

tinue to harass him. On May 15, 2007, Liu was assaulted
and detained by police while he was going to a birthday celebration. His family was threatened and told not to draw
public attention to his unlawful arrest. After being taken to
the police station for questioning, Liu was released later that
afternoon. Some of the arresting officers admitted that the
arrest was illegal, but they knew that if they let Liu go, they
would lose their jobs.

*Father, give us the courage to remember others who are imprisoned
and suffering, even if in remembering we suffer ourselves. May we
never become complacent about injustice, and may we always seek to
protect those weaker than ourselves who need our help.*

SOURCE: CHINA RIGHTS FORUM

MY HEART WILL SING

He doesn't know I serve You now

He must not see that I have found

A hope that's sweeter than this life will ever be

For years I've dreamed that it was so

A love that would not let me go

My life is changed

I have been ransomed by the King

With everything that's in me

I want to shout Your name

But here inside my heart

I must silently proclaim

Jesus

My heart will sing Your praises

And I won't be afraid of

What this life may bring

Jesus

With all that is within me

I'm living in this victory
You have won for me
And if the moment rises
When I must choose this life or
Choose the One who gave His life for me
Jesus, my Redeemer
I will gladly choose my King

All my chains are stripped away
In my heart You've etched Your name
A hidden rendering of this freedom I have gained

I can't believe You've chosen me
You helped my blinded eyes to see
Now I rest in every promise You have made

In this world I cannot
Lift my voice in praise
But here inside my heart
I am crying out Your name

SHANNON J. WEXELBERG,
FROM THE CD *BETTER THAN LIFE*

My Heart Will Sing

*I will be glad and rejoice in your love, for you saw my affliction
and knew the anguish of my soul.*

PSALM 31:7

In the Middle East, in the heart of Islamic belief, there is a country that is antagonistic to Christians. Bibles are not allowed. Worshiping Christ, even at home, isn't permitted. People are arrested for having private prayer meetings, for singing worship songs, and for teaching the Bible to their own families.

To put the intensity of this persecution in perspective, one father was arrested after his son turned him in to authorities for teaching his family about the Bible.

However, the gospel is penetrating this nation through missionary radio. Far East Broadcasting Company, HCJB Global, and Trans World Radio are proclaiming the gospel, and millions are hearing the message of hope. It's a message of freedom from the bondage of Islam.

The Islamic world allows women fewer rights than men regarding marriage, divorce, civil rights, legal status, dress code, and education. Some women aren't allowed to be educated past the eighth grade. They're forced to wear the burqa as a sign of modesty. Husbands are also permitted to admonish their wives by beating them.

Ana found Christian radio while seeking some comfort for her loneliness. She had never heard the name of "Isa" (Jesus) before. But she couldn't believe it when she heard that Isa loved her so much that He died for her sins.

In a country where women are viewed as second-class citizens, Ana's curiosity was piqued. She couldn't understand how any man would give her the time of day, let alone give his life for her. Ana continued listening to radio programs that told her that other women were having similar experiences.

As Ana listened to the programs of encouragement, she heard the clear gospel message and felt the call of God on her heart. She eventually gave her heart to Christ. Unfortunately, in this Muslim nation, that's a death sentence. Muslims who convert to Christianity are considered apostates. If they are found out, they're threatened with death.

Ana must keep her faith secret from her family and

community or risk this penalty, but she listens to the radio broadcasts as often as she can. She's growing in her faith and looks forward to her time of worship every day. She longs for the moment when her husband and children are away so that she can worship in silence. Yet even in her silent worship, her heart loudly proclaims her praises to Jesus. She lives in the victory that He has won for her. And should she ever have to choose between this life or the One who gave His life for her, Ana will choose her King.

Father, thank You that Your gospel is heard, even in places where great effort is made to silence it. Receive our praise and thanksgiving for the freedom and comfort we enjoy in You. Give us the courage to worship You alone.

SOURCE: MISSION NETWORK NEWS

It is impossible for a human heart, without crosses and tribulations, to think upon God.

To die for the sake of Christ's word is esteemed precious and glorious before God. We are mortal, and must die for the sake of our sins, but when we die for the sake of Christ and his word, and freely confess them, we die an honourable death; we are thereby made altogether holy relics, and have sold our hides dear enough. But when we Christians pray for peace and long life, 'tis not for our sake, to whom death is merely gain, but for the sake of the church, and of posterity.

FROM *THE TABLE TALK OF MARTIN LUTHER*

PERSECUTION WATCH: PAKISTAN

Ninety-seven percent of Pakistan's citizens are Muslim, and that makes the situation for Christians in that country precarious. In 1947, Pakistan was formed as the Muslim section in the partition of British India. For more than half of its history, Pakistan has been ruled by the military, deposing elected governments at will.

Christians face severe opposition from militant Islamic groups. They are regularly barred from jobs or face troubles from their employers and co-workers. Christian merchants are often harassed. The war in Afghanistan intensified problems, with Pakistani Christians seen as being a part of an attack on Islam.

In 1998, Sharia law was adopted in Pakistan, under which Christians have limited rights. Many Pakistani Christians have been falsely accused under a law that makes blaspheming Mohammed or the Koran a crime punishable by death. Even if acquitted, those accused often face threats, violence, and even death at the hands of mobs following their acquittal. While there have been proposed amendments to the law, they have had little effect.

Imprisonment, torture, and death surround the lives of Christians in Pakistan. In 2002, gunmen in Karachi executed seven Christians. Pastor Mukhtar Masih was murdered at a railway station in central Pakistan as he waited for a train; unidentified gunmen shot him twice in the chest. Gunmen killed Reverend Shamoun Babar, a Protestant minister, and his aide, Daniel Emmanuel, in 2005. They were presumably abducted, and when their bodies were discovered, it was evident that the men had been knifed and shot. Then their bodies were mutilated. Six Christians were injured and one Christian worshiper was killed during an Easter service when four Muslim gunmen, members of the Dogar family, opened gunfire. The church had already canceled its Good Friday and Saturday evening services because the Dogar family had threatened to kill anyone who came to the church.

In spite of opposition, the church continues to thrive in Pakistan. Pray that God would grant wisdom to Pakistani believers and comfort for those who have suffered or lost loved ones. Pray that in spite of all the hostility directed at them, Pakistani Christians will display the love of Christ to their Muslim neighbors.

SOURCE: MISSION NETWORK NEWS

Twisted Words

All day long they twist my words; they are always plotting to harm me . . . My enemies will turn back when I call for help. By this I will know that God is for me . . . In God I trust; I will not be afraid. What can man do to me?

PSALM 56:5, 9, 11

To be accused of the crime of blasphemy in Pakistan is a serious matter. In a country where 97 percent of the people are Muslim, there is little sympathy for the Christian population. Blasphemy cases can drag on for years, and appeals can take even longer. In the meantime, prisoners accused of blasphemy are treated inhumanely and are often beaten—and even killed—by the other inmates. The sentence for those convicted of blasphemy is death by hanging.

Pakistani citizen Ayub Masih, a Christian, was arrested in 1996 when he was twenty-six years old for allegedly blaspheming Mohammed in a private conversation with a neighbor. After the alleged blasphemy occurred, a mob of radical Muslims attacked Ayub and his brother and took them to jail. His brother was later released.

Violence and injustice characterized Ayub's imprisonment and trial. During the trial, religious extremists threatened to kill Ayub, his lawyers, and his judge if he were not convicted. (In 1997, a judge in another case was killed when he acquitted two men accused of blasphemy, so threats of this nature must be taken seriously in Pakistan.) In what would eventually be a six-year incarceration, there were two attempts made on Ayub's life, and once during his trial, his accuser shot at him outside the courthouse.

Finally in 1998, Ayub was sentenced to death for his "crime." Catholic Bishop John Joseph protested Pakistan's blasphemy laws and Ayub's sentence by shooting himself on the steps of the courthouse. The Lahore High Court upheld Ayub's sentence in 2001.

A courageous decision by Pakistan's Supreme Court in August 2002 acquitted Ayub Masih and ordered his immediate release. His life still threatened, however, by Muslim extremists, Ayub fled his native country and was granted political asylum in the United States. Remaining in Pakistan are his brother, who was seriously injured in the attacks af-

ter the accusation, and his elderly parents. In his new country, Ayub hopes to study English and become a minister.

*Father, thank You for Your grace and protection from those who
would twist our words and seek to do us harm. Help us to remember
that our trust is in You, and You are for us.*

SOURCE: MISSION NETWORK NEWS

Servant of All

Jesus said, "If anyone wants to be first, he must be the very last, and the servant of all."

MARK 9:35

Missionaries Martin and Gracia Burnham were committed to a life of service. They both had grown up in missionary families, and just two years after their marriage they went to the Philippines, where Martin, a pilot, flew passengers and supplies for New Tribes Mission. They lived and worked there for nearly twenty years with their three children.

Their greatest act of service began, strangely enough, in a beautiful Philippines resort where Gracia and Martin had gone to celebrate their wedding anniversary in May 2001. Shortly before dawn on the morning of May 27, Martin and Gracia were awakened by the sounds of men pounding on their door. Armed with M16s, Islamic Abu Sayyaf terrorists corralled the couple, along with twenty other hostages, into a speedboat and held them captive in the jungle at gunpoint for over a year.

Their time in captivity was horrifying. Martin was handcuffed and tied to a leash. Both Martin and Gracia suffered from intestinal viruses, malnourishment, and sores all over their bodies. Over the course of the year, the couple endured seventeen fierce firefights between their captors and those who attempted to rescue them. Gracia describes the experience: "You never knew when the gunfire was going to start . . . We would hear the bullets whiz past our heads and they would smack into trees." The couple was sustained through all of this by singing hymns, quoting Scripture, and praying—for their children and for their own release.

Martin viewed his situation as an opportunity to be a servant. Gracia recalls her husband saying that those who want to be great in God's kingdom must be the servant of all. Gracia recalls, "I watched him be kind to [the captors] and I just watched him be a servant and love them." Both Gracia and Martin shared the gospel with the terrorists.

During the course of the year, some of the hostages were released, and some were beheaded. By June 2002, Martin, Gracia, and a Filipina nurse were the only hostages left. On June 7, the hostages knew there would be another encounter with the military because they had been followed all day. When the rescuers opened fire, all three of the hostages were shot. Gracia was wounded in the leg, and both Martin and the nurse were killed. Martin and Gracia had said good-bye to one another many times during that year, but this time their goodbyes for this life were final.

Gracia was rescued and returned to her children. Recovered from her injury, she lives in Kansas in Martin's hometown. She believes that Martin is in heaven, a better place, and that God is good.

Father, help us to remember that You have called us to be the servant of all—not just of those who treat us well but even of those who would persecute us. May we always serve with kindness and willingly offer up the greatest kindness of all—sharing Your gospel.

SOURCE: MISSION NETWORK NEWS

We can always look at the experiences of our lives in the light of the life of our Lord Jesus, who "learned obedience," not by the things He enjoyed, but by the things He suffered. Was there suffering in His life? A great deal. Losses? All kinds. Was it His glory that was at stake? No, His single aim was to glorify His Father, and He did just that, every moment of His life . . .

He accepted suffering. He willingly laid down His life. He poured out His very soul unto death. Shall not we, His servants, tread the same pathway? . . .

There is nothing by which death can hold any of His faithful servants, either. Settle it, once for all—we can never lose what we have offered to Christ. We live and die in Him, and there is always the resurrection.

ELISABETH ELLIOT, *A PATH THROUGH SUFFERING*

A Life Saved

Whoever wants to save his life will lose it, but whoever loses his life for me will save it. What good is it for a man to gain the whole world, and yet lose or forfeit his very self?

LUKE 9:24–25

Daruka Abhi, a Gospel for Asia missionary in India, knows that even though life as a Christian can be difficult and filled with persecution, a life without Christ is long and full of torment. A group of anti-Christian extremists has targeted Daruka, a pastor in Maharashtra, his wife, and his child, threatening to kill them all if he refuses to renounce Christianity and return to his former religion.

Daruka trusts God, however, and he has no plans to meet the demands of the individuals making the threats. In his thirteen years of ministry, Daruka and his family have faced persecution, and they have remained faithful to God. Daruka remembers all too well what life without his faith is like.

Daruka was born to a high-caste, wealthy Hindu family in Bombay. When Daruka's mother became ill, his family had the financial resources to acquire the best medical treatment for her. But when civil unrest caused the banks to close, Daruka's family had no access to their money, and his family begged their traditional gods and goddesses to heal the ailing woman. Without medical treatment, Daruka's mother died, and he began seeking something to take away the pain of her loss. He sought comfort in illegal drugs, but when he found no peace, he concluded that he must end his life. Family loyalty caused him to change his mind, but in the meantime, Daruka decided there was no God.

Through the witness of one of Daruka's aunts and missionaries at her church, Daruka heard the gospel, and he finally found the peace in his heart he had been seeking. Daruka repented of his sins and asked Jesus to save him. Soon after, he felt called to the ministry. His immediate family was angry about this decision. "The result of my decision to follow Jesus yielded me nothing but a total boycott from the family and expulsion from the ancestral property, which I gladly accepted for the sake of following Christ," Daruka explained.

Daruka walked away from his family's wealth and placed his complete trust in God. But this was only the first time

Daruka's faith would be tried. A few years after becoming a missionary, Daruka and his wife and son were sharing the gospel at an open air meeting. Anti-Christian extremists broke up the meeting and attacked Daruka and his family. They destroyed the equipment, tore apart the gospel literature, and injured Daruka and his family so badly that it took them three months to recover from the injuries. A few months after the attack, Daruka had an opportunity to share the gospel with Waliur, one of the attackers. Waliur and his family became Christians, and the people in that village who saw the amazing change in Waliur's family eventually became Christians too.

In spite of the threats against his life, Daruka remains committed to reaching the dozens of surrounding villages and to planting at least three more churches in the area. He knows from experience the difference the gospel makes and that life without Christ is the greatest loss of all.

God, make us willing to lose our lives and find the salvation that comes only from You. This world offers us many things, but we know that without You, we have nothing.

SOURCE: GOSPEL FOR ASIA

Producing Many Seeds

Jesus said, "Unless a kernel of wheat falls to the ground and dies,
it remains only a single seed. But if it dies, it produces many seeds.
The man who loves his life will lose it, while the man who hates his
life in this world will keep it for eternal life. Whoever serves me
must follow me; and where I am, my servant also will be.
My Father will honor the one who serves me."

JOHN 12:24–26

When missionaries Nancy Mankins, Tania Rich, and Patti Tenenoff last saw their husbands Dave, Mark, and Rich on January 31, 1993, the men's hands were tied behind their backs as they marched into the Panamanian rain forest, the prisoners of armed guerrillas who had kidnapped them. The New Tribes Missions couples and their children served in the small village of Procuro, about fifteen miles from the Colombian border. Their work was translating the Bible into Kuna, a dialect spoken by about seven hundred people, and teaching the Indians who spoke the dialect how to read and write it as well.

On that Sunday evening in 1993, the families were settling into their routine—reading, conversing, putting their young children to bed. Guerrillas carrying automatic weapons burst into each of the homes and demanded that the wives pack a suitcase for their husbands with three sets of clothes. Nancy had the presence of mind to include a Bible, and Patti tucked a family photo into her husband's suitcase.

The next day brought action, as the missionary agency flew the families back to the United States and a crisis management team formed and sent personnel to Panama. It was determined that the men had been abducted by Revolutionary Armed Forces of Colombia (FARC) rebels, a Marxist-rebel group that controls about 40 percent of Colombia.

The rebels had stolen a radio preset to the mission's frequency, so they were able to communicate with the New Tribes Mission (NTM) crisis team. They demanded five million dollars, or the men would be killed. It was the mission's policy not to pay ransoms because it might make missionaries in other parts of the world vulnerable to terrorists who might have similar kidnapping strategies, and although the crisis team explained that these were not men of means, the kidnappers remained unreasonable in their demands. Demands, threats, "proof of life" messages, and deadlines came and went during 1993. The men sent a last proof-of-life message just before Christmas 1993, but by January 1994, guerrilla communication ceased.

The NTM crisis team got help from humanitarian organizations; the governments of the United States, Colombia, and other Latin American countries; and the news media. They followed leads and met with guerrilla agents, sometimes putting their own lives at risk in the hope of securing the men's release.

Over the next few years, NTM continued to make appeals and follow leads with guerrilla defectors. In 1994, two other NTM missionaries were kidnapped in Colombia; their bodies were found a year and a half later in the mountains north of where they were kidnapped. Guerillas again made contact with the crisis team in 1996, and hope for release was renewed. The sudden silence of the guerrillas in the middle of the year brought more confusion and disappointment. Among the accounts circulating among the tribal peoples was the rumor that the men had been killed; yet their deaths couldn't be confirmed.

Finally, in 2001, the leader of the crisis team met with a rebel defector who had once guarded the hostages. He confirmed that the men had been killed five years earlier. They had been executed during a military assault on the rebels, and FARC didn't want the hostages slowing them down as they made their escape. The remains of the men have never been found.

The "kernels" of these men's lives, however, have produced many seeds. Because of their work, Kuna people can now read about Jesus' love and offer of salvation in their own language. More than thirty Kuna churches rejoice in their freedom in Christ. And Nancy, Patti, and Tania remain NTM missionaries committed to evangelizing people in remote areas of the world who have not heard the gospel.

Father, sometimes we become discouraged because it seems that the losses we suffer for Your sake are meaningless. Help us to remember and be encouraged that we are kernels, and the works we perform in Your name will bear seed in due time.

SOURCES: NEW TRIBES MISSION, MISSION NETWORK NEWS

O COME, O COME, EMMANUEL

O come, O come, Emmanuel,
And ransom captive Israel,
That mourns in lowly exile here
Until the Son of God appear.

O come, O come, Thou Key of David, come
And open wide our heav'nly home
Where all Thy saints with Thee shall dwell—
O come, O come, Emmanuel!

Rejoice! rejoice!
Emmanuel
Shall come to thee, O Israel.

LATIN HYMN, 12TH CENTURY

On Earth Peace

*Glory to God in the highest, and on earth peace to men
on whom his favor rests.*

LUKE 2:14

Anything but quiet and understated, the Christmas season in Western countries is impossible to ignore, with displays of colorful Christmas cards, shiny ornaments, and artificial Christmas trees making their way into stores in early fall. Shoppers begin the countdown of how many days left until Christmas as soon as one Christmas season ends. The greatest threat to Christians living in these countries is that they will get lost in consumerism and forget to celebrate Christ's coming to earth. While some people would like to do away with the religious significance of the day—greeting acquaintances with "Happy holidays!" rather than "Merry Christmas!"—celebrating the birth of Christ involves no real threat to their well-being.

For Christians living in Muslim nations, however,

Christmas has become a day of anything but peace. Christians in Indonesia celebrate Christmas throughout the whole month of December. On December 5, 2003, a group of six Christians who were singing Christmas carols and playing their guitars outside their Indonesian Christian Church in Poso City found out that celebrating can be dangerous. Two armed men riding a motorcycle, carrying a military-style pistol, fired shots at the group, injuring two of the six people. The two did recover.

In Pakistan, a mob of armed men attacked a church near the Indian-Pakistan border on Christmas day, 2002. There were over a thousand worshipers inside the church attending services. The attackers set off several bombs, then grabbed valuables from the congregation and raided a church safe before fleeing. No one was killed in the attack, but several were injured.

In Laos, eleven Christians were arrested for holding religious services on Christmas day in December 2003. The group was finally released in mid-January 2004. Iraqi Christians, and Christians in other Muslim nations as well, refrain from public Christmas celebrations; they know that Muslims wanting to make a political statement often use this season of the year to do it.

We joyfully sing, "Peace on earth, and mercy mild," as we celebrate our Savior's birth, and while Christians in Muslim nations may sing these words as well, they realize that their celebration of that reconciliation between God and man may come with great cost to their physical lives. The hope of their Emmanuel sustains them in an environment of hostility and hatred.

Father, we thank You that You sent Jesus to earth to be our Emmanuel, "God with us." Even when the world around us may threaten us with conflict and violence, we thank You for the true peace that we have with You through Your Son.

SOURCE: MISSION NETWORK NEWS

Not only will I appreciate the scars of Christ [in heaven], but also the scars of other believers. There I will see men and women that in the world were cut in pieces, burnt in flames, tortured and persecuted, eaten by beasts, and drowned in the seas—all for the love they had for the Lord. What a privilege it will be to stand near their ranks! . . .

The Lord inferred that if His followers were to share in His glory, they would also have to share in His sufferings. And the deeper the suffering, the higher the glory. This is why the apostle Peter could say that to the degree one suffers, keep on rejoicing, *"Rejoice* that you participate in the sufferings of Christ, *so that you may be overjoyed* when His glory is revealed" (1 Peter 4:13). We rejoice on earth . . . so that we may be overjoyed in heaven.

JONI EARECKSON TADA, *HEAVEN: YOUR REAL HOME*

PERSECUTION WATCH: SAUDI ARABIA

When Islam gained control of Saudi Arabia 1,300 years ago, all Christians were expelled from the country. Considering itself the guardian of Islam's holiest sites, Saudi Arabia forbids all other religions.

Despite endorsing agreements on religious freedom and enjoying a favorable status with Western nations, Saudi Arabia has one of the world's worst human rights records. Any person involved in evangelism or who converts a Muslim faces jail, expulsion, or execution. Even visiting foreigners are not allowed to gather for worship.

It is clear that the Lord is at work in Saudi Arabia, even in the most difficult circumstances. Speaking to Compass Direct, Brian O'Connor, a Christian who spent seven months in prison in Saudi Arabia, was able to lead twenty-one fellow prisoners to faith in Jesus Christ. "I was there for a purpose," he testified. "And on the flight home [to India after his release], I shared with another man who prayed with me to receive Christ."

Since 1992 there have been more than 360 cases of Christian expatriates being arrested for participating in private worship. Despite this, the Defense Minister, Prince Sultan, told reporters in March 2003 that Christians are free to worship privately, but reiterated that no church buildings will be allowed. He said, "We are not against religions at all . . . but there are no churches—not in the past, the present, or future." With the death of King Fahd, persecution of believers has not improved, but has been on the rise under the new King Abdullah.

SOURCE: VOICE OF THE MARTYRS, CANADA

In Chains for Christ

I want you to know, brothers, that what has happened to me
has really served to advance the gospel. As a result, it has become
clear ... that I am in chains for Christ.

PHILIPPIANS 1:12–13

Brian O'Connor learned all about the risks of being a Christian in Saudi Arabia, one of the countries known for its persecution of Christians. In Saudi Arabia, all forms of religion except Islam are prohibited. The Muttawa, the religious police, actively seek out those guilty of possessing Bibles, crosses, and rosaries or of attending Christian gatherings. Although some Saudi princes have said that private gatherings are permissible, the Muttawa make no distinction between private and public meetings.

An Indian national, Brian arrived in Saudi Arabia in 1998 to work as a baggage handler for Saudi Arabian Airlines. He held private Bible studies in his home and owned nearly two hundred Christian DVDs and videos. He also had a digital Bible on his computer.

In March 2004, the Muttawa arrested Brian, and he was taken to a mosque where his legs were chained together and he was hung upside down. The religious police came in and took turns kicking, punching, and whipping him. His torture included being whipped on his back and the soles of his feet with electrical wires.

Eventually, the Muttawa took Brian to the police station and ordered that he be put under arrest on three charges: preaching Christianity, selling liquor, and peddling drugs. The Muttawa had no direct proof of their claims. While Brian admitted preaching the Bible, he denied converting Muslims to Christianity. The other two false charges—selling liquor and drugs—are frequently made against Christians suspected of spreading the gospel.

Brian's time in prison was miserable and frightening. He shared a cell with sixteen other criminals, including those convicted of murder and drug peddling. After Brian befriended several cellmates, they petitioned the jailer to allow him to pray, but only between the five daily Muslim prayers.

Brian was finally brought to trial in September 2004.

In the meantime, a campaign for Brian's release finally succeeded when the second-ranking Saudi prince ordered that all charges be dropped. But the court still tried Brian for alleged alcohol sales. He was sentenced to ten months in jail and three hundred lashes. The court counted the seven months he had already served, and Brian never received the whipping. One night he was taken from his cell and put on a flight to India, where he was reunited with his family.

Brian views his time in prison as a blessing. Through his ordeal, twenty-one people came to know Jesus, and his faith and endurance are stronger. Brian considers it a privilege to have suffered in the name of Jesus.

Father, help us see our trials as opportunities to advance the gospel. May our faith and endurance grow, and may we understand that our suffering is a privilege that we bear for Christ.

SOURCES: MISSION NETWORK NEWS, COMPASS DIRECT

PRAY

That I'll make the most of every opportunity
That I'll share my faith with all those in need
That the good news will go out to every nation
That chains will break and captives be set free

Pray
That I won't be afraid
That I'll call upon His name
In times of trouble
Pray
That I count it all a joy
To suffer for my Lord
Every day
Just pray

That I reach out with compassion for the broken
That I won't see my life as my own
That I will go wherever God would lead me
That I remember this world is not my home

For those who thirst
For those who hunger
That they find Living Water and the Bread of Life
And for the poor
And all those who suffer
That they may find their refuge in the Christ

Pray
That we won't be afraid
That we'll call on His name
In times of trouble
Pray
That we count it all a joy
To suffer for our Lord
Every day
Just pray

SCOTT KRIPPAYNE, FROM THE CD *BETTER THAN LIFE*

Pray

Is any one of you in trouble? He should pray . . . The prayer of a righteous man is powerful and effective.

JAMES 5:13, 16

A predominantly Muslim country, Tajikistan became an independent republic in September 1991 following the collapse of the Soviet Union. The fledgling nation was quickly plunged into a five-year civil war for control of the central government. Civil war was then followed by three years of drought and natural disasters. Life is difficult for all the citizens of this impoverished nation, but particularly tenuous for Christians living there. While religious freedom is protected in the country's constitution, militant Islamic groups prove a threat, and the government uses this threat to closely monitor religious practice.

Sergei Besarab was a missionary pastor in the northern Tajikistan town of Isfara. The Isfara region is generally considered more devoutly Muslim than the rest of the country, so Sergei faced great challenges in his mission work there. As a new Christian, Sergei had been trained by Bible Mission International to become a missionary. Sergei quickly earned a reputation as an active missionary; he became the pastor of a young church in Isfara and distributed Tajik-language leaflets to residents.

Struggles were not new, however, for Sergei. Before he became a Christian, he had served four prison terms for his involvement with illegal drugs. It was in prison that Sergei heard the gospel and converted. The leader of Tajikistan's Baptist Union explains that his group conducts services in prisons, and through their ministry, Sergei came to know the Bible and was born again. A Baptist pastor who knew Sergei as a prisoner testifies that he became a completely different person after his conversion.

On the evening of January 12, 2004, unknown assailants armed with automatic weapons burst into the yard of the Baptist church in Isfara. Sergei was on his knees praying and singing before a meal when the gunmen shot him through the window. When his wife, Tamara, heard the shots and rushed in from another room, Sergei was already dead.

A week before Sergei was killed, the local newspaper published an anonymous article sharply criticizing Sergei's missionary work and pointing out his four previous criminal convictions. A few months later, when members of an Islamist group were arrested as suspects in the murder, Isfara's mayor again attacked Sergei's work, suggesting that the killing was drug-related.

Although it was brief, Sergei's ministry was powerful and effective—so much so that his enemies believed that the only way it could be stopped was by killing Sergei.

Father, thank You for hearing us when we pray. Whether our lives are filled with trouble or with joy, may we always recognize the importance of praying to You.

SOURCES: MISSION NETWORK NEWS; VOICE OF THE MARTYRS, CANADA

Something to Drink

*Then the King will say, "Come, you who are blessed by my Father;
take your inheritance, the kingdom prepared for you since the
creation of the world. For I was . . . thirsty and you gave me
something to drink."*

MATTHEW 25:34–35

Missionaries Larry and Jean Elliott, Karen Watson, and David and Carrie McDonnall have left a legacy of love in Iraq. Four of the missionaries were killed March 15, 2004, when automatic weapons fire and rocket-propelled grenade fragments tore into the vehicle they were riding in; only Carrie survived, but with serious injuries. The team had been assessing water purification needs at an isolated camp of refugees in Mosul when the gunmen fired on them.

Veteran missionaries, the Elliotts had served for twenty-six years in Honduras. Larry and Jean touched many lives during their service in Honduras, and their ministry and work there contributed to the establishment of twelve

Baptist churches, ninety-two mission points, and eighty water wells. Larry will be remembered for his hearty laughter and commitment to the power of prayer, and Jean's smile and her desire to serve people living in places with great needs are her legacy. The couple believed that their service in Iraq was their calling, and despite the instability in that war-torn country, they were happy to be there.

Karen Watson was doing the job that friends say she was created for. Devoted to a life of service, Karen had joined the Southern Baptist International Mission Board in 2003. She worked in refugee camps in Jordan and Kuwait and eventually moved into Iraq to distribute food, set up water purification systems, and help the Iraqi people rebuild their lives. Other co-workers compared Karen with Tabitha, a woman in the Bible known for her deeds of kindness and charity.

David and Carrie McDonnall had been drawn to Iraq by their passion to share the good news of God's love with the Iraqi people. Both David and Carrie had experience as single missionaries in the Middle East, so they were aware of the dangers of working in the region. They had been married only a year when a team leader from a Christian organization suggested they consider working in Iraq. Although they knew that they might face danger, they believed that God was calling them to serve there.

Carrie suffered serious injuries during the attack, but she survived. She lost three fingers on her left hand, and shrapnel remains in her body. She misses her husband, but she has learned to trust God's faithfulness. She has shared her story in her 2005 book *Facing Terror* and through speaking at events, spreading her ongoing passion for missions and the gospel.

God, because of our love for You and our neighbor, may our works of service bring glory to Your name. May we leave a legacy of love, meeting the needs of the people around us in the place You have called us to be.

SOURCES: MISSION NETWORK NEWS,
INTERNATIONAL MISSION BOARD

The School of Suffering

Remember how you remained faithful even though it meant
terrible suffering. Sometimes you were exposed to public ridicule
and were beaten, and sometimes you helped others who were
suffering the same things. You suffered along with those who were
thrown into jail, and when all you owned was taken from you,
you accepted it with joy. You knew there were better things
waiting for you that will last forever.

HEBREWS 10:32B-34 NLT

From the first persecuted pillars of the church to modern day believers in China and other places all over the world, those who have suffered for Christ have testified that the school of suffering taught them lessons they could have learned nowhere else.

One imprisoned pastor from Vietnam still speaks of prison as a "special school." There he says he learned to live in hope for the same "better things" the author of Hebrews spoke about almost two thousand years ago.

MICHAEL CARD, *IN THE STUDIO* RADIO PROGRAM

Orphans and Widows in Distress

Religion that God our Father accepts as pure and faultless is this: to look after orphans and widows in their distress and to keep oneself from being polluted by the world.

JAMES 1:27

In 2002, Siham Qandah, a Jordanian Christian widow, was found to be an unfit mother to her two children, Rawan and Fadi, ages thirteen and twelve at the time. Siham's troubles began in 1994, when her husband, a soldier in the U.N. peacekeeping forces in Kosovo, died.

Legal struggles began when Siham applied to have her deceased husband's army benefits legally transferred to her and her children. When she submitted her application, she was surprised to find that the local Sharia court produced a document stating that her husband, three years before he died, had converted to Islam. The document bore the names of two witnesses, but there was only a scrawled "X" in the place where Hussam's (Siham's husband) name should have been.

Under Islamic law, however, if a father converts to Islam, his minor children automatically become Muslims; they could only receive their inheritance through a Muslim guardian.

Siham was advised that it would be hopeless to contest Hussam's alleged conversion certificate, so instead she asked her estranged brother, who had converted to Islam as a teenager, to serve as the children's financial guardian so that they could receive their benefits. Siham would retain legal custody of the children.

Siham's brother, Abdullah al-Muhtadi, began to keep some of the children's monthly benefits for himself, and after about four years of this, Siham began court proceedings to change the guardianship. In 1998 Abdullah filed a lawsuit demanding custody of the children so he could raise them as Muslims. He didn't want them attending the Christian school their mother enrolled them in, he claimed, and he wanted them to be raised with Islamic rituals and doctrine. He had seen the children once.

A three-year civil battle ensued. In 2001, the civil court awarded custody of the children to Abdullah. Siham appealed this ruling, but the court upheld it. Siham then appealed to the Supreme Court, but the case was rejected.

Advice from top judicial and religious leaders was for

Siham either to become a Muslim or leave the country. Her children, however, had been blacklisted on immigration computers, so she could not leave the country with them.

In October 2002, in an order issued by the ministry of justice, Siham was given five days to surrender her children or face imprisonment. Because of Siham's ongoing case to have her brother removed as the children's guardian, though, the order to arrest her was suspended. A nightmarish journey through the court system followed, but Siham finally triumphed in April 2005 when the Amman court of Islamic law revoked Abdullah's legal guardianship and ordered him to repay the misspent funds to the orphans' trust accounts.

God cares for widows and orphans, and He answered the prayers of this persecuted family by allowing them to remain together.

Father, we want our religion to be pure and faultless. Give us compassion for widows and orphans and others around us who are suffering distress. Protect them from those who would take advantage of them.

SOURCES: MISSION NETWORK NEWS,
CHRISTIAN SOLIDARITY WORLDWIDE

Because of Righteousness

Blessed are those who are persecuted because of righteousness,
for theirs is the kingdom of heaven.

MATTHEW 5:10

Peru, South America's third largest country, is besieged by political upheaval. Though Peru is touted to have the second most powerful armed forces in South America, the last several years have seen its army struggling to return to its right objectives, corrupted by the lure of easy money from drug traffickers.

David de Vinatea, selected as one of the ten best infantry Special Forces officers, was sent into the jungle to fight against guerrillas and drug dealers in 1994. The first thing he did on arrival at his command post was to put a sign on his office door that read "God rules this base." When the brigade general later visited, he told David to take it down, saying, "In this army, I rule!"

Seven months into David's tour of duty, forty drug dealers were arrested, six large illegal landing fields and several drug laboratories were destroyed, and more than $280,000 was confiscated and returned to the National Bank. But a high official was not happy. With fabricated charges, he was able to get the courts to sentence David to sixteen years in prison, ending November 19, 2011. (Later, David discovered that this official had some arrangements with the drug lords.)

An international coalition spearheaded by Open Doors International interceded on David's behalf. It was to no avail. Many prayers were offered on David's behalf. As difficult as his ordeal was, though, David found some good in his prison experience: "Prison is where I really searched for God, because He is the Master of my life, and it was there where I came to know Him in His true dimension. I learned to pray for real."

Then, in 2000, President Fujimori fled from Peru. With the new government, David's sentence was commuted, and he was finally released from prison on November 19, 2003.

Today, David serves with RBC Ministries in Peru. His desire is to reach others for Christ, especially those in the armed forces. And through David's military friends, RBC Ministries has now been given an opportunity to place

God's Word, through *Our Daily Bread,* in the hands of all the soldiers in the Peruvian army.

Father, give us strength to make righteous choices, even when it would be easier and more profitable—in the world's eyes—to do the wrong thing. Remind us that when we are persecuted for righteousness, we have Your kingdom to look forward to as a reward.

SOURCE: RBC MINISTRIES

In 1956, five young missionaries were martyred in the jungles of Ecuador when they were attacked by a group of Waorani tribesmen that they were trying to reach with the gospel. The story shook the world. The following is the reflection of Elisabeth Elliot, widow of martyred missionary Jim Elliot, from her book about the incident, Through Gates of Splendor.

To the world at large this was a sad waste of five young lives. But God has His plan and purpose in all things. There were those whose lives were changed by what happened on Palm Beach. In Brazil, a group of Indians at a mission station deep in the Mato Grosso, upon hearing the news [of the killings], dropped to their knees and cried out to God for forgiveness for their own lack of concern for fellow Indians who did not know of Jesus Christ. From Rome, an American official wrote to one of the widows: "I knew your husband. He was to me the ideal of what a Christian should be." An Air Force Major stationed in England, with many hours of jet flying, immediately began making plans to join the Missionary Aviation Fellowship. A missionary in Africa wrote: "Our work will never be the same. We knew two of the men. Their lives have left their mark on ours."

PERSECUTION WATCH: AFGHANISTAN

Afghanistan is no stranger to struggle. The Soviet invasion in 1978 brought disaster, but the Soviets' pulling out a decade later did not bring peace to the war-torn country. When the Communists lost power in Afghanistan, Muslims took their place and engaged in a civil war—an Islamic jihad, or holy war—that degenerated into a cruel contest for religious and political supremacy between Islamic factions. The Afghan people were left to pick up the shattered pieces of their lives, leading to rule by the Taliban and its extreme form of militant Islam. Under the Taliban, there were extremely stringent rules—women were no longer allowed to attend school or hold jobs, and men had to adhere to a strict Islamic code. Non-Muslims were denied freedom of assembly, and open profession of faith in Christ among refugees often led to death. Converts to Christianity were often killed by their own families.

Under the U.S.-led war on terrorism, the Taliban government was overthrown, leading to a new interim government. With this change, there is new hope but also continued concern about religious freedom during this transition and into the future.

The year 2004 saw a shift in policies and governing authorities in Afghanistan. A new constitution was adopted in January, and in October of that year, Hamid Karzai became the first democratically elected president. There continue to be concerns the constitution is somewhat vague in policies relating to religion, which could lead to abuse of minorities in the future.

Unfortunately, the Taliban still maintains a strong influence in areas that are not under the strict control of government rule, and its iron fist was seen in July 2004 when Taliban guerrillas claimed responsibility for cutting the throat of a Muslim cleric after they discovered he was propagating Christianity. Taliban spokesman Abdul Latif Hakimi told Reuters in a telephone conversation that a number of foreign aid agencies were likewise involved in spreading Christianity and would face a similar fate. "We warn them that they face the same destiny as Assadullah if they continue to seduce people," he said.

The Taliban makes no idle threats. In July 2007, the Taliban abducted twenty-three South Korean Christians. The group, made up mostly of female nurses and English teachers in their twenties and thirties, came to Afghanistan for a ten-day medical missions trip. On July 30, the Taliban shot and killed two members of the group because it was not satisfied that its demands for the release of twenty-three Taliban prisoners and for the withdrawal of South Korean troops from Afghanistan were receiving attention. Two female hostages were freed on August 13, and in late August, South Korean negotiators secured the release of the remaining nineteen. One of the conditions of release: South Korea would stop its nationals from doing missionary work in Afghanistan.

Human rights leaders pressed the Afghan government in 2006 over the case of Abdul Rahman, who was charged with apostasy after he converted from Islam to Christianity. Rahman faced the death penalty if he refused to become a Muslim again. The case was dismissed when Rahman was deemed mentally unfit to stand trial, and he ultimately found refuge in Italy from those who still wanted him killed.

Muslims make up the vast majority of the population. Christians make up only 1/100 of 1 percent of the population, and there are still eighty-eight unreached people groups in this nation. Christians in Afghanistan often suf-

fer verbal abuse and intimidation, beatings, loss of employ-
ment, and imprisonment. Christians endure a harsh life in
this ultraconservative Muslim country.

SOURCES: MISSION NETWORK NEWS;
VOICE OF THE MARTYRS, CANADA;
NEW YORK TIMES, JULY 26, 2007

Jars of Clay

We have this treasure in jars of clay to show that this all-surpassing power is from God and not from us. We are hard pressed on every side, but not crushed.

2 CORINTHIANS 4:7-8

Both Dayna Curry and Heather Mercer realized that they could serve God best by sharing His love with others. He didn't require extraordinary talents, gifts, or achievements—just their willingness to serve the poor and love their neighbors. This realization and their desire to serve God overseas brought Dayna to Kabul, Afghanistan, in 1999 and Heather in 2001 to do full-time relief work with the organization Shelter Germany.

Their work came to a halt, however, on August 3, 2001, when Taliban guards carrying rifles and whips arrested them as they came out of a home where they had just shown the *Jesus* film to a family they had befriended. Six other foreign Shelter workers and sixteen Afghan employees were also arrested that day. They were charged with proselytizing, which carries a penalty of death for Afghans and imprisonment or expulsion from the country for foreigners. In an interview, however, an Afghan judge commented that the Shelter Now foreign workers, if convicted, would be sentenced according to Sharia law, which requires a penalty of imprisonment or hanging.

After the initial arrest, the Taliban interrogated the Shelter workers for twenty-two hours and then locked them into their cells in a rodent-infested cement building. The prisoners were treated well by their captors and were allowed to visit with their families on several occasions in late August and early September. The International Committee of the Red Cross was permitted to visit with them as well. A trial seemed to be under way.

Then the terrorist attacks against the United States happened on September 11, 2001, and the trial was postponed indefinitely. The prisoners were transferred to a maximum-security prison in Kabul a week after the attacks on the United States. When anti-Taliban Northern Alliance troops and U.S. air strikes seemed to be weakening the Taliban stronghold, the prisoners were moved to another abandoned prison eighty miles from Kabul.

The day the prisoners arrived at their final place of imprisonment, American bombs were falling near the building. Heather, Dayna, and the rest of the Shelter Germany workers feared they might become casualties of war before they ever had a chance to be tried and sentenced. When a soldier ran into the compound announcing that they were free, the prisoners celebrated with the liberated citizens dancing in the streets. Later, Heather and Dayna were rescued from a dark field by a U.S. Special Forces helicopter.

Back in the United States, the two women became the focus of media attention and had many opportunities to share the story of their work in Afghanistan, their prison experience, their release, and the Christian beliefs that motivate them. They wrote a book, *Prisoners of Hope,* and recorded a CD of praise songs they wrote and sang while in prison. They continue to serve the people of Afghanistan through the foundation they established, the Hope Afghanistan Foundation.

God, make us willing to serve You, even though we are weak. Help us to remember that even though we are only jars of clay, we hold the treasure of Your gospel and Your love.

SOURCES: MISSION NETWORK NEWS

On the suffering of Jesus and the victory He accomplished:

No one has suffered more unjustly at our hands than this sinless God-Man, and yet he was "delivered up according to the definite plan and foreknowledge of God" (Acts 2:23). We can be assured that in the crises we face, large and small, God works all things together for good (Romans 8:28) because God's strength has once and for all been made perfect in weakness. The unity of God's sovereignty and goodness that will be fully disclosed on the last day has already dawned decisively in the work of Christ. God has triumphed over the serpent, sin, death, evil, and tragedy. "It is finished!" Jesus cried. Our victory is assured, though we walk through the valley of death's shadow (Psalm 23:4). In fact, in this famous psalm of comfort in distress, we can say, "I will fear no evil, for you are with me; your rod and your staff, they comfort me."

MICHAEL HORTON, *TOO GOOD TO BE TRUE*

More Desirable Than Gold

The laws of the Lord are true; each one is fair. They are more desirable than gold, even the finest gold. They are sweeter than honey, even honey dripping from the comb.

PSALM 19:9–10 NLT

Most of us take for granted the copies of the Bible we have in our homes and churches. But for people like Fiodor, who lived in the Soviet Union during the Cold War, the opportunity to worship in church and possess a copy of God's Word are rich blessings to be treasured.

When Fiodor was a boy, he noticed that his mother would take him and his siblings to the government-allowed Central Moscow Baptist Church, and while his father came along on occasion, he often went elsewhere on Sunday mornings. Fiodor began to ask his mother why his dad didn't come with them, but she ignored his question. Fiodor persistently asked, and finally his mother shared a secret that he was not to repeat to his friends: his father was pastoring an underground church in a village a couple of hours outside of Moscow.

One Sunday Fiodor accompanied his father to the village church, which was held in a home. The service was a typical worship service, but Fiodor noticed a couple of things. The people sang quietly, and most of the elderly people that made up the congregation had tears running down their faces during the service. Fiodor asked his father why they were crying, and his father explained that it was because they were so happy to have this time with the Lord. And they were also praying—asking God to give them the freedom to worship without the fear of being imprisoned.

Through the years, Fiodor watched as his father was arrested several times. Eventually his father was sentenced to three years in a military camp for his Christian beliefs, his preaching, and for being one of the leaders of the underground church. Fiodor and other members of his youth group would visit the small groups that made up the underground church outside of Moscow, and the elderly people would cry with joy to see that the church would continue in Russia with the next generation.

As a college student, Fiodor learned what it meant to be

persecuted for his faith when a teacher asked him to stand up during class. She asked him if he was a Christian and a Baptist, and when Fiodor answered that he was, the teacher and the rest of the class mocked him. Some of the students in the classroom refused to be his friend.

After college, Fiodor went into the obligatory military service. There were no Christians with whom he could fellowship or pray. Fiodor had no Bible, and he got the message to his brother that he desperately needed one.

Interestingly, at the same time, an American couple, Brent and Cindy, who were traveling to the Soviet Union, took their permitted four copies of the Bible into the country, hoping to leave them with Christians there. Brent attended the Moscow Baptist Church and slipped one of his copies to a man in attendance there. With a joyful expression on his face, the man accepted Brent's gift and quietly slid it into his jacket. This gift would become a treasured possession for Fiodor.

When Fiodor received a package from his brother, he found Brent's Bible hidden in the box lid. He was overjoyed and began crying. He was thrilled to finally have God's voice speaking to him through His Word. Fiodor hid the Bible in his right boot. At times he had to swim with it and walk with it in the snow and rain, but he managed to protect his treasure, pulling it out to read when he was by himself in the woods or the restroom. His copy of the Scriptures saw him through his military service.

When Fiodor traveled to the United States in 1995 to attend seminary, he still had his treasured Bible with him. He shared his testimony one night at a church in Arkansas, and the pastor noticed that one of the pages had a U.S. address written on it. Through that address, the pastor contacted Brent, whose trip to the Soviet Union had occurred ten years before. Brent and Fiodor met and became friends, and Brent was thrilled to hear how his simple gift had enabled Fiodor to survive and grow spiritually while he was in the military.

Fiodor now works with the Russian Baptist Union and coordinates ministries, helping to establish Sunday schools, medical missions, and a radio ministry in Russia. He also helps plant new churches in the United States among Russian-speaking people.

Father, may we always realize what a treasure we have in Your Word. Help us to remember the needs of our brothers and sisters in

*other parts of the world who don't have this blessing and work to
make Your Word available to them.*

SOURCE: *WORDS TO LIVE BY*

FAITH OF OUR FATHERS

Faith of our fathers, living still
In spite of dungeon, fire and sword—
O how our hearts beat high with joy
When-e're we hear that glorious word!

Our fathers, chained in prisons dark,
Were still in heart and conscience free;
How sweet would be their children's fate
If they, like them, could die for Thee!

Faith of our fathers, we will love
Both friend and foe in all our strife;
And preach thee too, as love knows how,
By kindly words and virtuous life.

Faith of our fathers, holy faith,
We will be true to thee till death!

FREDERICK W. FABER

PERSECUTION WATCH: YEMEN

Strategically located along ancient trading routes, Yemen is one of the oldest civilizations in the Middle East and was the ancient home of the Queen of Sheba who traded gifts with King Solomon. Modern-day Yemen was formed out of a merger of two distinct republics in 1990, the northern republic practicing a form of Shiite Islam known as Zaydism and the southern republic predominantly Sunni Muslim. Islam is the official religion, and the legal system is based on Sharia law.

Before Muslims overran the country in the seventh century and cut off nearly all outside influences, there was a significant Christian population. Today Yemen is one of the world's least evangelized countries, and the few Christians living in Yemen are not allowed to witness. It is illegal to convert from Islam.

Because there is such a small number of Christians (estimated at 0.05 percent of the population), their walk with Christ is difficult due to discouragement and isolation from other believers as well as the threat of significant societal pressure. Most Christians are foreigners working in the country and many are Ethiopians.

Because of the U.S.-led war on terrorism, Yemen has been cracking down on supporters of al-Qaeda in the country. However, there remains a significant element of militant Islam in the country. On December 30, 2002, a Baptist-run hospital was attacked, and three foreign missionaries were killed. The attacker testified in court that he did it out of religious duty, "in revenge for those who converted Muslims from their religion and made them unbelievers." Local residents denied that the American missionaries were involved in trying to convert people to Christianity.

SOURCE: VOICE OF THE MARTYRS, CANADA

The Death of His Saints

Precious in the sight of the Lord is the death of his saints.
O Lord, truly I am your servant.

PSALM 116:15–16

Jibla Baptist Hospital in the nation of Yemen has provided medical care and extended the love of Jesus to hundreds of thousands of people since missionary doctor Jim Young established it in 1967. Yemen is a poor, conservative Muslim nation in the Middle East, and the dedicated people who have worked there since the hospital's inception have faced many challenges through the years, including wars, fires, political and legal pressures, financial and personnel crises, and even kidnappings. But on December 30, 2002, Dr. Martha Myers, administrator Bill Koehn, purchasing manager Kathy Gariety, and pharmacist Don Caswell faced the greatest challenge possible.

On a Monday morning, a lone gunman gained entrance to the hospital by cradling his gun inside his jacket as though it were a sick child. He went into a room where Martha, Bill, and Kathy were meeting with other staff and opened fire. Martha was killed immediately, while Bill and Kathy died soon after. The gunman then shot Don, who was working in the pharmacy, seriously injuring him. Don later recovered from his wounds. After the Islamic gunman was arrested, he told police that he carried out the attack in service to Allah.

The three victims have left an amazing legacy. Dr. Martha, well loved by the Yemeni people, had come to the hospital as a career doctor in 1978 and never considered doing anything else. Besides her work at the hospital, she visited people in their homes, befriending many. She drove to isolated Yemeni villages, where she did community health work and immunized many children.

Administrator Bill Koehn led the hospital for twenty-eight years. The Yemeni people remember him as a man who made wooden toys for children in an orphanage he loved to visit, assisted the needy widows of the community, and showed concern for the struggles and needs of the Yemeni people. His widow, Marty, returned to serve at Jibla after his death.

Both Bill and Martha knew the risk of serving in Yemen,

a nation where Islamic radicalism has taken hold. They had both expressed their desires to be buried in this country that they loved. Their side-by-side graves rest on top of a hill overlooking the hospital compound, a tribute to the love and compassion of Christ exhibited in their lives.

Father, even though we are saddened when people we love die, we know that Your servants' deaths are precious to You. Please make us willing to serve You so that others see our love for You, in life and in death.

SOURCE: MISSION NETWORK NEWS

THE PLEASURE OF MY KING

What a joy to serve my King
Walk the path of suffering
Whether free or bound in chains
I will spread Your fame

There are hearts inside these walls
Spirit, You have heard them call
You have sent me to this place
A prisoner of Your grace

So pour me out
Like sweet perfume
There are souls
In need of You
Have Your way
O, Christ in me
For I serve at the pleasure of my King

Though my path is filled with thorns
I delight in You, my Lord
For Your Word has been my light
Shining pure and bright

It's for love You brought me here
There is nothing that I fear
For in death or in my life
You'll be glorified

Not my will but Yours be done
Here on earth, Your kingdom come

SHANNON WEXELBERG,
FROM THE CD *BETTER THAN LIFE*

The Pleasure of My King

I am suffering even to the point of being chained like a criminal.
But God's word is not chained. Therefore I endure everything for the
sake of the elect, that they too may obtain the salvation that
is in Christ Jesus, with eternal glory.

2 TIMOTHY 2:9–10

Sometimes what humans intend for evil, God uses to accomplish good. Missionary pastor Manja Tamang is learning this lesson as he serves a twenty-year sentence in a Nepali prison for a crime he did not commit.

Manja served Christ wholeheartedly in a small mountain village in Nepal as a pastor and evangelist. One day when Manja was doing ministerial work, he made a discovery that would change his mission field. While he was walking along a path, he found a dead body, and Manja reported his finding to the police. An anti-Christian group in the community that opposed Manja's work also found something that day: an opportunity to frame Manja for the crime.

A few days later, the police arrested Manja for what they determined was a murder. They gathered "evidence" from his home—clothing they claimed belonged to the victim. During Manja's trial, false witnesses came forward to testify against him. The victim's widow protested, saying that Manja was innocent, but the court found him guilty and sentenced him to twenty years in prison.

All of this happened seven years ago, in 2000. Manja's supporters fought the conviction for two years, and eventually his case went before the Supreme Court. In spite of tremendous evidence proving Manja's innocence, the court upheld the sentence. Manja remains in prison.

But "God's word is not chained." Those who falsely accused Manja, hoping to squelch his ministry, have not been successful. Rati, Manja's wife, remains faithful to her husband, visiting him in prison, praying for him, and caring for their two children. She reaches out to her community with the gospel, teaching kindergarten, serving on an outreach team, and working with her church's women's ministry.

And Manja has found a new mission field. While his separation from his family is sad and the injustice he has experienced is discouraging, he continues his witness for Christ. He believes that God is sovereign and that he has been chosen, as God's servant, to be put in prison. God has blessed Manja's work. He holds Bible studies for fellow prisoners who want to learn about Jesus, and more than thirty-five have become Christians. Prison wardens have been impressed with Manja's character and have appointed him as a prison medical assistant. He also has completed an education degree while in prison.

Although it would be easy for Manja to despair and become bitter, he has chosen to "endure everything" with trust, faithfulness, hope, and love. Manja serves at the pleasure of the King.

Our King, You are the sovereign One who can bring good out of evil, and so we serve wherever You are pleased to place us. Help us to remember that Your truth is more powerful than human lies, Your freedom releases us from earthly chains, and Your love drives away our fears.

SOURCE: GOSPEL FOR ASIA

Mission Groups and Ministry Support Organizations

These mission groups and organizations serve God's people throughout the world. They have contributed to the stories featured in Better Than Life.

Every Child Ministries

Every Child Ministries shows the love of Jesus to the neediest of African children in practical ways and teaches African nationals to train their own people through mercy ministries to homeless street children, through seeking to release and retrain slave children, and through medical and rehabilitation ministries to the sick and handicapped. For more information, contact ECM at P.O. Box 810, Hebron, IN 46341 or at http://www.ecmafrica.org

Gospel for Asia

In each aspect of Gospel for Asia's ministry, the primary aim is to plant churches among the unreached—those who have never heard the gospel. Gospel for Asia trains and sends native missionaries because they have proven extremely effective. For more information, contact GFA at 1800 Golden Trail Court, Carrollton, TX 75010 or at http://www.gfa.org.

Hopegivers International

Hopegivers International, a faith-based, not-for-profit humanitarian agency, provides "help for today and hope for eternity," rescuing homeless children, widows, the sick and needy. For more information, contact Hopegivers at P.O. Box 8808, Columbus, GA 31908 or at http://www.Hopegivers.org

I.N. Network

The mission of the I.N. Network is to connect front-line and supply-line partners in effective evanglism, discipleship, and community development to glorify God and win men, women, and children to Jesus Christ. For more information, contact I.N. Network at 10432 Chicago Drive 2, Zeeland, MI 49464-8370 or at http://www.innetworkusa.org

International Mission Board

IMB leads Southern Baptists to be on mission with God to bring all peoples of the world to saving faith in Jesus Christ. For more information, contact IMB at P.O. Box 6767, Richmond, VA 23230-0767 or at http://www.imb.org

Mission Network News

Mission Network News is a mission news service dedicated to keeping Christians informed on evangelical mission activity around the world; in doing so, MNN hopes to educate and motivate Christians to prayer, participation, and support of missionary work to help further the Great Commission. For more information, contact MNN at 1159 East Beltline Ave. NE, Grand Rapids, MI 49525 or at www.mnnonline.org.

New Tribes Mission

NTM coordinates missionaries, sent by local churches, to take the gospel to tribal people. Missionaries then plant churches. They disciple believers, translate the Scriptures, and train teachers and leaders, who in turn reach out to their own people and to neighboring tribes. For more information, contact NTM at 1000 East 1st Street, Sanford, FL 32771 or at http://www.ntm.org

Open Doors with Brother Andrew

The action of Open Doors ministry includes delivering Bibles, training materials, physical needs, and other help to believers living in restricted countries worldwide. Open Doors' calling especially includes the training of pastors and church leaders in evangelism, equipping them to effectively proclaim the gospel of Jesus Christ. For more information, contact Open Doors at P.O. Box 27001, Santa Ana, CA 92799 or at http://www.opendoorsusa.org

The Voice of the Martyrs, Canada

The Voice of the Martyrs exists to serve the persecuted church through helping those who suffer for their faith, remembering the families of today's Christian martyrs, rebuilding the church's witness after persecution ends, reaching out in love to the persecutors, and raising a voice for those who cannot speak. For more information, contact this organization at P.O. Box 117, Port Credit, Mississauga, ON L5T 1Y6 or at http://www.persecution.net

The Voice of the Martyrs, USA

Voice of the Martyrs has been actively serving the persecuted church for almost thirty years. The Voice of the Martyrs was founded by Pastor Richard Wurmbrand, who spent fourteen years in prison for his activities in the Romanian underground church. For more information, contact VOM at P.O. Box 443, Bartlesville, OK 74005 or at http://www.persecution.com

Words to Live By

Since 1995, RBC Ministries' *Words to Live By* has told inspiring real-life stories of faith from around the world. This weekly radio program shares the personal stories of how God's Word changes hearts and lives. Visit *Words to Live By* on the Internet to find out which station airs the program in your area, or listen online at http://www.words.net

World Evangelical Alliance

World Evangelical Alliance exists to foster Christian unity and to provide a worldwide identity, voice, and platform for evangelical Christians. Seeking empowerment by the Holy Spirit, WEA extends the kingdom of God by proclamation of the gospel to all nations and by Christ-centered transformation within society. In 1996, WEA began the International Day of Prayer (IDOP), a global day of intercession for persecuted Christians worldwide. Today, IDOP is the largest prayer-day event of its kind in the world. For more information, contact WEA at 13351 Commerce Parkway, Ste. 1153, Richmond, BC V6V 2X7 or at http://www.worldevangelical.org.

Note to the Reader

The publisher invites you to share your response to the message of this book by writing Discovery House Publishers, Box 3566, Grand Rapids, MI 49501, USA. For information about other Discovery House books, music, or videos, contact us at the same address or call 1-800-653-8333. Find us on the Internet at http://www.dhp.org/ or send e-mail to books@dhp.org.

SONGS CELEBRATING TODAY'S STORIES OF FAITH

Featuring the passionate voices of:

Shannon Wexelberg, Scott Krippayne, and Charles Billingsley

**San Diego Rescue Mission
120 Elm Street
San Diego, CA 92101**

Here's your chance to be inspired and make a difference in someone else's life. *Better Than Life* has ten songs drawn from the real-life stories of modern men and women, Christians from around the world, who have suffered for Christ. Your own faith will be challenged and encouraged, helping you not only to praise God, but praise Him through all of life's struggles.

What's more, a portion of every sale goes to international missions to help spread the timeless truths of God's Word around the world.

Be inspired, and help inspire others to come into God's kingdom.

SONG LIST: Better Than Life • Count It All Joy • My Heart Will Sing • Send Me • The Pleasure of My King • These Scars • Pray • Stand Strong • To Live Is Christ • Willing

Prices subject to change without notice.